In Living Memory

A collection of contemporary visual arts, original essays,

poetry, and first-hand memories of those

who survived the war years

Curated by Olympia McEwan

BLUE
ORMER

Published by Blue Ormer Publishing, 2020.
www.blueormer.co.uk

All contents remain the copyright of the contributors, © 2020.
This collection curated by Olympia McEwan.

Cover design by Ryan Morley.
Front cover:
    'Homecomer story, dedicated to Beda' by Olympia McEwan.
Rear cover:
    photography by Graham Jackson.

ISBN 978-1-9993415-7-2 (Hardback)
ISBN 978-1-9993415-4-1 (Paperback)

Printed by Short Run Press, Exeter.

*All proceeds of the book, after costs, will go to **Age Concern** in Guernsey and Alderney. The aim of the charity is to promote the welfare of older people in Guernsey and Alderney, to increase public awareness of the issues concerning ageing and encourage positive attitudes towards the older members in our community.*

Contents

Foreword

There are still many islanders who remember May the 9th 1945, when the bells of the Town Church rang out after five years of silence. They remember singing 'Sarnia Chérie' to mark the arrival of the British liberating troops. A day that would from then on be known as Liberation Day.

In reality, islanders could fly their flags from 3.00pm on the previous day, May the 8th, and many turned on their hidden radios in order to listen to Winston Churchill.

Many stories have been published over the years. This latest, *In Living Memory*, captures those never-before-documented memories. Indeed, some have never been told until now – seventy-five years later.

Those treasured memories have been brought together with feeling, by artists, authors, poets, historians and, of course, the survivors. That is exactly what occupied islanders did for five long years: they survived and became the bedrock of a strong Guernsey. A community which has led us all into the twenty-first century.

Within this book there are heartfelt stories of those who stayed in Guernsey, and equally emotional stories of those who had to leave without knowing when – or if – they would return. There are works that describe the separation of families and friends, whether that be in Guernsey, Alderney or Sark. *In Living Memory*, tells the different experiences in words, pictures and paintings: together commemorating the freedom that we all enjoy today.

Dame Mary Perkins

(photos by Grant Dowinton)

Preface

In Living Memory has been created by a community of specialists in their various fields, for an audience of outsiders as well as enthusiasts. All of the material in this book is original and the majority of it has been created specifically for this project. The purpose of this book is to re-present the subject of the Occupation of the Channel Islands to a new audience, as well as bringing to light new material, to shed further light on the complex world experienced by these brave few.

I am not a specialist in this subject. However, my intention was to seek out those who are, to gain a better understanding and, in turn, take the reader on a journey. I am an artist and I have a passion for people and their stories. My interest lies in the social history of the occupation – the lived experience of this last generation of survivors. I also felt that this project was time-critical, as those with first-hand experience of the war years are becoming fewer in number.

As an outsider, I have felt deeply moved by those I have met, who were so graciously generous with their time and desire to share their narrative – giving further clarity to the wider picture of the occupation of the only territory in the British Isles to be invaded and occupied by German forces during WW2. As I trace the arc of the progress of *In Living Memory*, my understanding of this fascinating and haunting period reveals itself to me. I hope you will also experience a journey of your own as you spend time with these amazing works of art, stories and essays.

The essays written by survivors have never been published before. The other survivor stories I have written as monologues. I have tried to stay true to each individual's voice, using their own words taken from the transcripts of our recorded conversations.

There are many people to whom I am indebted. I am especially grateful to those who gave their time, knowledge, and skills to this book – starting with all my wonderful contributors, without whom this book would not exist.

I would like to thank my publisher, Steve Foote, who took the reins very late on in the process, and whose reassuring counsel helped me believe in my mission. I would like to thank Claire Allen, Director of Guernsey Literary Festival, for her enthusiasm from the start and for her kind introductions. Thank you to Michael Williams for his passion for

the subject and his assistance with reading material, as well as his kind introductions. I would also like to thank Celia Allen, the Very Rev Tim Barker, Rev Jan Fowler and Anne-Isabelle Boulon of Alderney Visitor Information Centre for their assistance during my visit to Alderney. Thank you to Richard Heaume (owner of the German Occupation Museum), Elmarie Brache for liaising with the artist Molly Harris, Lisa Todd for her publishing advice, Kim Bell for her introductions and to the photographers Paul Chambers and Graham Jackson for their assistance with the high-quality images we can now enjoy in this book.

Thank you to Molly Bihet for her very warm welcome into her home and to her daughter Carol for assisting with the introduction to this book. Thank you also to Ryan Morley for helping to create the cover design, and to Anna Smith and Debbie Torode for their awesome typing skills. Debbie, I hope your ears have recovered! Thank you to Jane Moss and Mary Carey for their eagle-eyed proofreading and a big thank you to Bianca Sarafian for her much-appreciated fresh approach to the project.

And finally, I would like to say a massive thank you to Dame Mary Perkins, for supporting and sponsoring the printing of this book. Two years ago we met for a chat about my various projects. She asked if I might like to create a book about the occupation as this is a subject very close to her heart. The idea did intrigue me, as I had recently created a portrait on an occupation theme, which had sparked my interest in the subject. I decided that if I were to embark on such a challenge, it should be ready for the 75th anniversary of liberation. I love to work to a deadline, and there could be no better objective than this.

And here we are, in the year 2020! I am elated to present to you this original and inspired publication. I hope you enjoy reading and looking at it, as much as we all have enjoyed creating it.

Olympia McEwan

(photo by Paul Chambers)

Introduction

Seventy-five years ago Guernsey was liberated from Nazi rule after five long, stark years of occupation. I was very honoured and pleased to be invited to write the introduction to this special book to celebrate the anniversary of Guernsey's liberation.

Olympia McEwan has coordinated this book which recalls the hardships of many throughout the occupation, celebrates our liberation and the joyous times throughout the year 1945, and demonstrates Guernsey's resilience. Olympia has drawn contributions from talented local artists, poets, local and renowned authors and historians, as well as personal accounts of survival through the occupation.

I was growing up from age nine to fourteen years during the occupation, and living with my family in our town house overlooking the sea and harbour. My memories are well recorded within the four books I have written about that time, and I believe that if we had not been living at Rose Villa, I would not have such interesting stories to write about. We were all so grateful for my grandfather's act of resistance in hiding his gun, which was not discovered during the house searches. My mother also shrewdly outwitted the Germans by faking an illness and collapse during a house inspection, which enabled us to stay in our home throughout the five years. Many islanders told me their own occupation stories after I published my first book in 1985, *A Child's War*. I then wrote about those stories in my subsequent books.

I can hardly believe it was seventy-five years ago that Guernsey was liberated from Nazi Occupation. It is of course vitally important that we keep memories alive of this momentous time in Guernsey's history for future generations. In spite of terrible hardship and fear that they lived under, local people went out of their way to ensure that others were safe and fed. The occupation years of 1940 to 1945 were very dark and troubled years, but the people of Guernsey came together and helped each other through to liberation. That shared experience has greatly influenced how we have lived our lives personally and shaped the island's character in the years since then – as illustrated in Olympia McEwan's *In Living Memory*.

This book will be a fitting keepsake for this special time of 2020, celebrating seventy-five years of freedom. Sarnia Chérie!

Molly Bihet

Richard Guille

Final Witnesses: Memories of the German Occupation of Sark, 1940-1945

On 10 May 1945, the Channel Island of Sark's tight-knit community was liberated by British forces from nearly five years of German Occupation. The release from the repressions, deprivations and uncertainties of the war years was a momentous and joyful event for the islanders. A letter written in May 1945 by Bertie Falle, a Sark hotelier, indicates this: 'What a day [liberation] was, all Sark turned out … and what a cheer we gave the boys, we all went nearly mad, singing shouting and some crying with happiness'. Sark's liberation put the dark years of occupation in the past and many Sarkees sought to close the door on a period which they wished to forget. As Gee Guille, an eighteen-year-old in 1945 remarked of her parents, 'it was over and done with, they were living again.' However, the occupation was never forgotten for the Sarkees and the event continued to shape their identities. Only a small handful of Sarkees remember the event today, many were children at the time and a few were in their mid to late teens. Their recollections of the war represent a last direct link to that period, what it was like to experience and what the event meant to those who lived through it. Between 2013 and 2016, I conducted interviews with Sark residents who remembered the occupation. The process was an intensely personal journey. My grandfather was born in 1942 and his parents endured the occupation on Sark, struggling to make ends meet whilst raising, feeding and clothing their four children. Their success in overcoming the challenges of occupation is testament to their resilience and inner strength. This was the fragmented family story which formed the basis of my understanding of Sark's occupation. Speaking to those who remembered

Sark's war years was a privilege, as the partial family story swelled into a far larger picture of a stoic, tight-knit island community enduring the most disruptive and challenging experience of its history with humanity, resourcefulness and resilience. This article reflects on the memory of the German Occupation of Sark, using the oral testimony of some of those who experienced it.

The importance of witness testimony is made all the more vital by the fact that Sark bears few obvious physical traces of the German presence. Unlike the other islands which were heavily fortified and left with large numbers of bunkers, gun emplacements and observation towers, Sark's high cliffs and lack of sites for amphibious landings meant that it escaped this fate. Resultantly, physical traces of the occupation are more subtle, from the rusting barbed wire posts recycled in fences by enterprising landowners, to the absence of sails on the mill, removed by the Germans to create an observation and machine gun post. The railings on La Coupée, the isthmus of rock connecting the two parts of Sark, were built by German prisoners of war, their role in its construction commemorated by a small plaque. Despite a small 'boom' in commemorations since 2015, with memorials to Sark's deportees and two British Commando raids on the island having been erected, Sark, as noted by Gilly Carr in 2014, does not have an extensive culture of memorialisation in comparison to Guernsey and Jersey. Resultantly, official narratives are more challenging to divine. Therefore, the voices of those who lived through the occupation enrich our understanding of how ordinary islanders experienced the event and what it meant to them.

On 3 July 1940 three German officers arrived on Sark to formally occupy the island. Initially occupied by a dozen troops, the German garrison swelled dramatically with companies undertaking three-month tours on the island. The numbers in comparison to the population were stark. In August 1941 there were 467 residents of Sark; by May 1945, with the population reduced by evacuation and deportation, 373 remained with a garrison of 270 German soldiers. This resulted in spatial integration, and some were removed from their homes to make space for troop billets, whilst others saw their properties pulled down on tactical grounds. From mid-1942 German doctors and medical orderlies administered treatment to the civilians, carrying out their duties with commendable professionalism and care. The islands' rural nature and agricultural tradition meant that Sark weathered the food shortages comparatively well, however the size of the garrison strained resources and the occupation was characterised by deprivation. Increasingly restrictive German orders and regulations, such as the imposition of a nightly curfew, created a sense of repression and uncertainty, exacerbated by the deportation of sixty-six islanders to internment camps in Germany in September 1942 and February 1943. As the occupation wore on, the islanders' freedom of movement was increasingly restricted through the laying of 13,000 anti-personnel mines and the wiring off of the centre of the island around the German headquarters. The minefields led to Sark's worst wartime tragedy, when four-year-old Nanette Hamon was killed whilst playing with her brother and cousin, an event which shook the tight knit island community. Overall, Sark survived the occupation well, much of this down to the resilience of the islanders and the leadership of the island's feudal Seigneur, the Dame of Sark Sybil Hathaway's firm leadership and hard line on the occupying Germans.

One of the central experiences of the occupation was hunger and deprivation. As the German presence grew, pressure on resources became increasingly acute, this only being marginally alleviated by infrequent supplies from France. In June 1944 when German supply lines were cut following D-Day, shortages grew parlous and both occupiers and occupied began to approach starvation. The islanders were helped by the much-awaited arrival of Red Cross food parcels which arrived in Sark on 3 January 1945 and at intervals afterwards. Moreover, fuel was increasingly rationed and became almost unobtainable by the winter of 1944/45. Clothing, footwear and medical supplies also grew scarce. On 29 May 1945, Hathaway wrote to friends in England summarising Sark's experience. She stated that 'by the time the first Red Cross supplies reached us in January, we were in a bad way. … The workmen had no boots and many of the children were almost barefoot.' Memories of deprivation and hunger were prominent. George Guille, a young boy at the time, could 'remember howling because we didn't have enough food.' His older sister, Elizabeth, told me how she'd 'seen my mother put food on the table for my father and the children and not have anything herself.' Memories of hunger and the relief of the food parcels left a lasting impression. Peter Carré, five at the end of the war, vividly remembered the Red Cross parcels: 'If I close my eyes and breath in, I can still smell the inside of the cardboard box of that Red Cross parcel.' Whilst the children were sheltered from starvation by their parents, memories of parental strain and severe hunger were strong. Others remembered the shortages of clothing, notably the wooden sabots which appeared on Sark and clothing recycled from curtains and bedsheets.

Pride is felt by those who lived through the period for the ingenuity and resilience of the islanders. People came together in the face of the shortages, in keeping with the strong sense of community. Esther Perrée, a teenager during the occupation, recalled how her mother would set aside valuable food to gift to a neighbour. She related how 'Everybody helped one another in those days …

nobody would let anybody go without something.' Communal bonds generally grew stronger during the occupation, and those who remember the deeper sense of community felt during those years do so fondly. Islanders went to great lengths to preserve a sense of normality, with a variety of ersatz substitutes being used, such as acorn coffee. Jenny Baker, a child of seven in 1945, related the improvisation her mother showed in providing a Christmas treat for her children. 'My mother made little round bits of butter where she'd gathered the cream from the milk we had, and she wrapped those up and they hung on the tree as gifts.' The shortages and memories of these continue to impact on the islanders. Few of those who experienced the occupation are wasteful, particularly in relation to food; severe hunger taught its value. Some recalled their parents lecturing them, when young appetites grew fussy, on how they'd have appreciated the rejected food during the war. Margaret Guilliard, a teenager during the occupation, remembered the food shortages well. She continued to remember the lessons she learnt during the war for the remainder of her life, and took pride in the collective achievement in weathering the deprivations. In 2016 she explained to me that 'We never waste anything. You're very careful and we still are to this day. And I always think if there was another war, we could manage. When you've had to, it's amazing what you can deal with.'

The defining feature of the occupation was the presence of the German soldiers. Islanders initially viewed their arrival with trepidation, notably those old enough to have remembered the First World War and the seventeen men of Sark who had lost their lives. Some, such as the Englishwoman Julia Tremayne, loathed the Germans throughout and deeply resented their presence. However, negative preconceptions created by British propaganda were quickly dispelled by close contact with the enemy, leading some to take a more objective view. Frances Pittard, who assisted British Commandos who raided Sark on the night of 3 and 4 October 1942, was questioned about conditions by the officer commanding the raid, Major Geoffrey Appleyard. The deportation of nine English born residents had occurred six days earlier, an action which seemed senseless and cruel to the islanders. Yet Pittard's responses to Appleyard indicate a balanced view of the enemy, even in light of their recent crime against the island community. Appleyard's report quoted Pittard as saying 'we are very bitter with the Nazis, but not with the Germans on the island.' Contemporary examples indicate that during the occupation, the Sarkees distinguished between the ideology that had brought the soldiers to their island and the men themselves.

Nevertheless, none of the islanders wished to be occupied and all resented the presence of the Germans. There was much Sarkian defiance, often low-level owing to the impossibility of armed resistance. This served as a way of keeping up morale and reminding the Germans of where the islander's loyalties continued to lie. The Sarkees frequently found ways to circumvent German orders. Perrée described how her mother and herself on their Sark farm would half-milk cows in front of the Germans requisitioning the milk, who not knowing any better would leave satisfied, giving Perrée the opportunity to keep some extra for herself. Despite the banning of radios in June 1942, many Sarkees retained sets or illicitly listened to the BBC news on crystal sets, taking part in one of the most widely engaged in forms of resistance to German rule as identified by Gilly Carr, Paul Sanders and Louise Willmot in 2014. The local patois was deployed by the Sarkees to converse around the Germans and, in some cases, to safely mock them. Sark's fishermen routinely engaged in a form of defiance which became local legend. Following escapes from Guernsey, fishermen had to take an armed German in the boat when they put out to sea. Bas Adams, a boy of seven at the end of the war, went fishing with his uncle and grandfather and recounted to me his memories of them deliberately making the

Germans sick in rough weather. 'I used to go with them, I was only tiny and he'd say "oh he's going to be sick today."'

The German soldiers who garrisoned Sark generally behaved well. Based on conversations with repatriated deportees, the London-based charity the Friends of Sark, formed to raise money for the island during the occupation, reported in 1944 that 'German behaviour was on the whole correct … instances are quoted of consideration being shown to the islanders.' However, Sark did not completely escape the harsh realities of German Occupation. Several islanders were arrested and imprisoned for breaking German regulations. When the German doctor was murdered by a fellow soldier in April 1942 all Sark men had to report twice daily to the German headquarters and all properties were roughly searched, until the soldier responsible was found. One Kommandant, Hauptmann Johan Hinkel, was so disliked for his involvement in the 1943 deportation that after his death in the same year, as Gee Guille stated, 'we were all celebrating because the Germans hated him and so did we.' Conversely, many of the low-ranking soldiers recognised that their posting to Sark was a blessing as opposed to more dangerous fronts and saw little point in causing trouble. Werner Rang, a German medic born in 1920, did two tours on Sark. His father had served in the First World War and had given his son advice on being an occupier: 'if you occupy another country, please be nice to the people of that nation. They don't want you to be there, and you don't want to be there either, but if you exercise a pleasant behaviour you will be accepted.' Werner won many admirers amongst the Sarkees for his professionalism and gentle nature, having put his father's advice into practice.

The good conduct of many soldiers of the garrison was remembered by the islanders. In the 1960s, Michael Marshall conducted research on Sark's occupation, recording conversations with a number of islanders.

One, Charles Perrée, reflected that: 'we can't blame 'em forever. There's some we'll always hate … and there's some Jerries too, if they came back to Sark, we'd smile and raise our caps.' Those who I interviewed remember the Germans from a young person's perspective. Esther Perrée told me, 'I remember my mother always saying "don't hang around chatting but always be very polite, say morning and afternoon, no more than that."' However, they did not share the fears of older generations, as the German soldiers generally were fond of Sark's children. Phyllis Rang, a woman in her early twenties at the time, explained how the soldiers 'spent their time giving the children rides in the car, they were always thrilled to bits with the children because some of them had children of their own.' Baker lived on a farm with her family. A German soldier assigned to the farm made Baker's younger brother a wooden dachshund. Baker reflected kindly on the soldier: 'he didn't want to fight, he didn't want to leave his family, so what do you do? You talk in pidgin English and pidgin German, don't you? … It was a sign of a type of friendship. It wasn't fraternising with the enemy; it was mere circumstances which required you to live together.' Such interactions led to an understanding outlook on the part of the Sarkees after the event. There is one factor above all others that ensured that the Sarkees remembered their occupiers in a manner which looked past the uniform. In 1949, Werner Rang returned to Sark married to Phyllis. Correspondence between the two whilst Werner was a prisoner of war turned a platonic relationship romantic, as Werner had fallen in love with the island and the woman who had worked as his medical interpreter. He immersed himself in the community, becoming a much-cherished member. Werner passed away in 2018 a year after Phyllis. During his life he served as a reminder for the Sarkees that many of the occupiers had been ordinary men who did not want to be there. This created space for a less partisan view to develop. Harriet Carré, a young mother during the war, wrote in the early 2000s about her attitudes towards the enemy:

'We have now had time to reflect, and realise that what we were asked to face up to was soldiers obeying orders.'

The occupation occurred at an early stage in the lives of those I have interviewed from Sark. The youngest were shielded from the worst parts of the experience by their parents. Baker argued that 'we didn't really realise what was going on … it was the norm. It was only once [the Germans] had gone and once we'd heard about the war that as we grew older, we realised the enormity of the occupation.' Despite this, the event impacted upon all and continues to shape their identity in the present. Growing up and living with older residents who had experienced the brunt of the occupation further shaped their views. Baker demonstrated this when recalling a batch of soap brought to Sark from France, which was rock hard and produced no lather. Such a small happening had a long-term influence. As Baker told me, 'I still have that bar of soap … I use it as a paperweight to remind myself of the privations!' The bar of soap became an object of memory, symbolising the experiences of her parents and her recollections of childhood under occupation. Others remember the deprivations by continuing to be conscious about not wasting food, everyday behaviour which stems from the collective experience of German occupation. The Sarkees had a nuanced view of their occupiers during the war and time for the older generations healed much lingering resentment. The younger members of Sark's wartime generation continue to hold these attitudes, being keen to emphasise the nuances of the human side of the event. For the interviewees, Sark's survival of the occupation was a source of pride. Phyllis Rang exemplified this when she reflected upon the culture of mending through the example of her mother teaching her how to recycle cotton thread from an old sheet: 'Can you imagine anyone doing that today? We knew and we could do it all again my generation.'

~ ~ ~

This article is for all those on Sark who shared their stories with myself, dedicated in particular to those who have passed away since I began this research in 2013.

Mavis Lemon

Taken from a conversation with Olympia and written as a monologue in Mavis' own words.

I was born in 1930 and lived on Sark with my family. I'll be turning ninety this year. In 1940 I would have been ten years old. There are a few things I can remember – my problem is that after the war we were advised to forget it all. So it's difficult to recall a lot of those memories now.

It was a tough experience but I've had a lot of good ones since. I've had a lovely life and I've been very lucky. The war experience taught us basic things, like respect for other people, the importance of a loving family, there were awful things that happened but you learned acceptance, because you didn't have a choice.

My strongest memory was from when I was twelve years old. I was sent over from Sark to Guernsey because at that time we had no doctors or dentists and I needed to be seen by a dentist. You had to get permission from the Germans to travel, which I did. And I ended up getting stuck over here and had a really bad experience. I was staying with a friend of the family, I'd been to the dentist and our friends had to drop me off at the Weighbridge. I had to have a German guard with me for the boat trip back to Sark and a special permit to travel. Their boat was flying the swastika and when I got onto the boat there was a raid on the harbour. It was either the Brits or the Americans, I'm not sure which.

I was actually on board at the time. I was put in the Captain's cabin, I believe. I could see the German guards had taken off their hand grenades and these things were all on a shelf in front of me, in the ship's cabin. Then the bombing started. I heard planes and everybody was running. I didn't know what to do, and in fact it was a German that took me by the arm, and hid me in their air raid shelter on the White Rock (which was knocked down after the war). It was terrible. There was an awful lot of noise and after the raid the skipper of the boat and everyone went back on board. It was a German who actually looked out for me and saved my life – I'm convinced of it.

There is one other incident that I can remember as a personal experience. I nearly killed a German! One summer they allowed us to go for a swim down at Grande Grêve, by the Coupée. They would take all the mines up for that particular day and we would go down the steep cliff path, down to the bay. We'd have a swim, there were probably nine or ten of us, and the German soldier would wait for us all. Once we'd had our swim,

15

we would make our way back up the cliff path. It had been a hot summer that year and the ground was very dry. My foot must have slipped and I released a great big boulder which rolled down the cliff and hit the German on the head! I was petrified and I thought I'd killed him. He was actually bleeding, the blood was pouring down his face. I don't think he realised what had happened. But it was me and I've lived with that thought all of my life. I nearly killed the poor man.

But you know, the ordinary German soldier was fine. They didn't want war, they didn't want to be parted from their families, it was the SS we feared. But you never quite knew who the SS were, so you had to be very careful.

My father was, I'm sure, a secret member of GUNS but he's never been mentioned in any records. He had horses and carts and he would do all the carting for the island. You had to have permission to go down to the Creux Harbour during the war, not everybody was allowed down there. So he would bring the news up from the harbour onto the island from the cargo boat. Do you know about GUNS? The Guernsey Underground News Service.

He would know which basket of tomatoes the news would be hidden in. We were never allowed to say anything about it and I can remember him telling us – 'I'm doing this but if you ever talk about it, we will all be shot!' Hubert Lanyon would then do the distributing of the news around the island. His daughter and I were the best of friends and we never ever spoke about it.

You know, we had nothing and times were hard. We were all loyal and in the end we were all just Sarkees together

getting by. There were no English people at all, they'd either left or they'd been sent to camps. A lot of our friends were sent away. We ourselves were on the list to go. My father wasn't a Sarkee but my mother had a heart problem and the Germans needed my father to work for them. So he was useful to them because he had a horse and cart.

We were four kids and how they ever fed us I don't know, but they did. My mother used to make lots of soup, to fill us up. Mum and Dad obviously gave us their rations and had nothing for themselves some days. My father was a big man but by the end of the war he weighed seven stone. He was giving us all he could. We had a field and he kept all the seed potatoes and he would dry out the broad beans and the peas, but sometimes food would go missing. By the end of the war the Germans were worse off than we were.

All the Sarkees stuck together and had as much fun as we could, and we did! I can remember going to the dances at the Old Hall with just a solo pianist for music. Oh dear, I can remember having no shoes. I didn't have any shoes at all to go to the dance, but my auntie had a pair of her own. So I would have to go over there every week and ask her to borrow them. You see, we used to walk about barefoot in those days. It was a harsh time and I think as a mother and grandmother now, I cannot imagine what my parents must have gone through.

Towards the end of the occupation we were all given a Red Cross parcel and my mother would take away the things that we couldn't eat, like soup, but there were tins of chocolate and she would say, 'You can either eat it all at once or keep a bit for every day, it's up to you. It's yours!' I remember opening a tin of chocolate once and there was a huge maggot inside. I shouted, 'Oh Mum look!' and she said, 'Oh baa... that's nothing!' She squished the maggot and got a knife, scrapped around the hole and said, 'That'll be fine now.' I also remember after the war, when we had our first loaf of bread, it tasted like cake!

I can also remember my dad bringing home a bucket full of salt water and we would forage, not on the cliffs because they were all mined, but we would go and get gorse to make a fire and my mother used to reduce the salt water, the salt would accumulate around the basin and that's how we made our own salt. We'd just have to make do. But we were never ill. I wasn't ill until after the war. We were catching measles and chicken pox and all sorts after the war had ended.

You know, when we knew the Germans were coming to Sark, our parents got us all together, all four of us, and said, 'Would you like to go with the school? What do you want to do?' We all wanted to stay with Mum and Dad, there was no way we wanted to go. But that's how we handled it as a family, we all stuck together. And we were very close. Had we gone away, who knows what would have happened..

My mum did some amazing things with the carrageen moss. We used to collect this special seaweed for her. Most of the beaches were mined, so we had to have a German with us the whole time. But we got used to them. I was doing my exams one summer, my German exams, and I remember sitting outside on the lawn with my books. One day this German soldier came over and told me he had a daughter of the same age and asked if he could help me pass my exam. So you know, there were good things that happened as well. I had an idyllic childhood really, in a loving family and we all got on and helped one another.

I do remember though when there were curfews especially after the German doctor was found murdered. This was during the summer and the curfew was from six o'clock every evening. So to pass the time we were all taught to knit. We used to unravel old jumpers and made our own jumpers from the recycled wool. I still knit to this day. I can't sit and watch television without the old needles going. And we were taught to patch and mend things. Imagine patching a pair of trousers today, you wouldn't do it would you, you'd go and buy another pair. My aunt used to make us summer dresses with curtain material and they were really lovely. But the only problem, as far as I was concerned, was that my older sister and I were always dressed alike. So of course when I'd outgrown mine, and she'd outgrown hers, and I used to have her hand-me-downs, so I ended up with a double whammy... But that's how it was and I just accepted it.

There it is, it was an experience, and it's certainly taught me a lesson in life – I know what it's like to go without. Everybody in Sark was very close, we were all in it together. You had to learn to appreciate everyone and everything you had.

Olympia McEwan

Barefoot but we ... keep smiling through

Mavis Lemon was born in Sark and lived through the occupation years with her extended family. They had to make do with what they had and she remembers being barefooted at times.

She and her sister were dressed in clothes made from curtains. If Mavis wanted to go to the weekly dance, she'd have to borrow a pair of shoes from her aunt. Times were hard, but they drew strength from knowing that they were all in it together – and were always there for each other.

'Barefoot but we ...
keep smiling through'
Olympia McEwan
Mixed media
133CM X 75CM

Diana Nicole

An Emotional Severance

Daddy's tears coursed down his cheeks as I waved good-bye from the back of Grandpa's car. I couldn't remember ever seeing a grown-up cry, and the sight of my tough, sports-mad father in tears was utterly astonishing. Now, in retrospect, I have to wonder if he had a premonition of what was to come? That the anticipated three weeks or so of separation might stretch to much longer. Could any of the ancient Greek playwrights have written a more

harrowing emotional drama than enacted in reality by the evacuation and occupation of Guernsey? Act One: The Desperate Decision: to stay and face an unknown fate at the hands of the enemy? Or to abandon home, business, possessions – all life as one knew it, to be looted and destroyed? Whether to send a beloved child on an enforced holiday for an unspecified period of separation, or keep the family together to face possible starvation or worse? So many decisions were made and reversed hour by hour. Act Two: The Exile and Entrapment: the frustration and numbing effect standing alone among strangers, yearning for the warmth and comfort of home, loving parents and things familiar or the aching void, the longing for sight and touch of lost children. Of deprivation and starvation. Act Three: The Final Tragedy: when the exiles returned, unrecognizable. The moment when the parent realized with horror that the lost child would never return, but was replaced by a premature adult with whom the loving relationship had been permanently severed. The moment when the Exile's excitement of stepping onto the homeland dockside was shattered by the expression of amazed disillusionment on the parents' faces.

Of course all good plays are interlaced with comedy and laughter. In the beginning there were hundreds of suitcases filled, never to leave the island: and men who determinedly saw their wives and children onto a ship – then failed to disembark themselves before the ship sailed. There were politicians exhorting the population not to be Yellow: 'don't be rats deserting the sinking ship,' and who then fled. We tend to view the present of our daily lives as through a telescope, isolated incidents enlarged and encapsulated, unrelated. The effect of time and distance constantly widens our field of vision so that an overall panorama emerges, each cause, occurrence and effect becoming a tiny tile fitting exactly to form life's magnificent mosaic. Now, after more than half a century, the tiles are all in place and we who were there can stand back to view the overall picture, no longer afraid to admit our own emotions, our parents safely beyond the reach of possible offence.

Pre-war my life was full of love, affection and sunny days (I don't ever remember it raining). The youngest grandchild by nearly a decade on my father's side, and the eldest on that of my mother. I was surrounded by grandparents, aunts, uncles and cousins, lively and affectionate, congregating every weekend for beach picnics, Christmas and Easter for celebrations and for every birthday and anniversary in between. Despite being an only child I was not spoilt: a strict code of discipline was enforced by a slapped bottom. A 'stiff upper lip' was demanded (no tears or whining allowed) and characters were judged by whether a person was a good sport, played fair at life as well as games. Every evening when Daddy came home he opened his coat wide to encircle Mummy and me in his huge embrace, with the dog skipping and yapping round our legs, wanting to be part of the action.

On June 19th, 1940, a month after my tenth birthday, Daddy brought home with him a silver identity disc on a chain, which he fastened round my neck. Having chosen to sail off on a huge adventure with my school friends, I failed to comprehend the significant glances exchanged over my head. I am sure many of us have recorded similar experiences of the evacuation: the waiting, the meals, the labels tied to our buttonholes. We remember the farewells to our parents, our choice of favorite book or toy to take with us. A myriad details remain clear to me – Daddy's tears for a start. On board the boat I shared a bunk with Pat and Monica Young, and we giggled hilariously when a stout lady in our tiny cabin, removed her dress and clambered up onto the top bunk in vast pink rayon bloomers with elastic holding them round her knees! After rolling at anchor for 12 hours, waiting for a pilot to lead us through the minefields into Weymouth Harbour, we British Citizens were herded into an empty cinema for examination that we were FFI (a military term for Free From Infection)! Then to the railway station. All I knew about trains I had gleaned from reading about Wells Fargo being attacked by men with feathers in their hair, galloping after us on their mustangs across the English countryside. I tried bravely to conceal my fear. The train steamed on into the night and we arrived in Oldham at 4am. Even in daylight, it was a very gloomy place, only glimpses of sky seen between the high, soot-blackened buildings. Amazingly, the people in Oldham did not have bathrooms in their homes. All sixty of us Guernsey Ladies' College girls were obliged to walk in 'crocodile' through the streets to a bath house where people used baths in rows of separate cubicles like public lavatories. After three weeks sleeping on horsehair mattresses on a Baptist Chapel Schoolroom floor, and having succumbed to tears in the dark just once, we were taken on a very long bus journey into the Derbyshire Hills, the fresh air and freedom almost like a home from home. Well, almost.

Lacking books and blackboards, our teachers had a hard time keeping us gainfully employed. We climbed up onto the moors, fossil-hunting, walked to the village of Windmill to buy knitting wool and needles for dolls clothes (not my scene) and played games in the garden where it never seemed to rain. A letter from my parents, mailed just before the Germans arrived, eventually caught up with me. I tried very hard not to succumb to tears. I recall the misery of blisters, like so many of the girls, on the back of my neck caused by the paraffin-soaked turbans we were obliged to wear day and night for weeks to kill off the head-lice, caught from the train, bus or horsehair mattresses.

The Florence Nightingale Memorial Home (built to accommodate elderly gentlefolk) in which we were lodged, was modern, comfy and the food was good. The Ladies' College Staff were kind and the sun continued to shine. All that was missing was love and affection. That problem was solved at my first billet in Denbigh, North Wales where we were taken by coach that September. I was swept into the arms of three generations of family all crammed into a tiny house on a street corner – a house full of love and laughter, strictly ruled by Taid (grandpa) with repeated references to The Good Book. 'Thou shalt do no manner of work on the Sabbath' (other than cooking the Sunday lunch) was the first rule. Not that there was much chance, what with school Church Parade to St Mary's Anglican Church in the morning, Sunday School at the Welsh Presbyterian Church where I was obliged to take the Oath of Abstinence (which I have ignored all my life) with Iain and Myfanwy, the grandchildren of my own age, in the afternoon. We attended Capel Mawr in the evening with the entire family, the only occasion when Nain (grandma) took her curlers out and put her teeth in. I was very happy there until a visiting cousin complained to my grandparents (who were elderly, unwell and living in lodgings near Hereford), that I was living in a slum!

I had enjoyed bathing in a tin tub on the flagstone kitchen floor with Myfanwy, and thought having to share a bed with her when extra family were visiting, was great fun! And Nain was a far better cook than my 'sports-mad mother' had ever been. Sadly, my cousin – and my fierce grandmother – won, and I was transferred to a magnificent country mansion. My grandmother and Aunt Doris had travelled 250 miles north to inspect my new billet. Enormously impressed by the long avenue of beech trees and manicured lawns, the oak-panelled drawing-room and the lady-of-the house who, though not titled, looked and spoke like a grand duchess. They waved goodbye to me from their taxi, well satisfied with the success of their trip. Little realizing that 'milady' had already pulled the tapestry bell-rope beside the fireplace, to summon her personal ladies' maid, to usher me away through the green baize door at the rear of the grand entrance hall, into the servants' quarters.

Fortunately I was joined by a school friend, Elizabeth, but we were obviously an added burden to Wilbraham, the black-clad ladies' maid, who sat at the foot of the large table in the servants' hall opposite Mrs Ball, the cook, with the pantry maid and the chambermaid opposite us. A chill atmosphere of protocol always pervaded this large room which overlooked the extensive fruit and vegetable garden, where we 'lived', and did our homework. Of course materially we lacked for nothing: food was good, fresh and plentiful, clothes laundered and repaired, stout country footwear provided. We trekked one and a half miles across fields to school every morning regardless of weather, until winter snow topped our high boots. Week-ends were a great joy: together with the cook's son, Bobby, we made camps in the woods, fished in the river and explored sheep tracks in the hills. We were taught how to saddle the donkey or harness him into his cart, and the cook would prepare us a hamper of food for day-long excursions. A children's paradise?

Elizabeth was lucky: her parents had escaped the island and were living near Devizes, so she received weekly letters from them. However, I did appreciate being able to visit my maternal grandparents and two of my unmarried aunts for most school holidays. This entailed train journeys to Chester, on to Shrewsbury and then on to Hereford. At first a member of staff accompanied us to Chester and saw us onto our various ongoing trains; but by the time I was twelve, I had charge of three or four juniors. The trains were full of soldiers and their kit bags, filling the corridors, over which I had to lift each child when she needed the loo! The boys in uniform were very helpful, passing her from hand to hand over their kit bags down each corridor and back to our eight-seater compartments.

Aunt Audrey, whom I adored, had often come to stay with us at L'Ancresse when I was a child. She had a very bad heart and so was never able to 'go out to work', but was sweet, affectionate and loved reading to me. Aunty Doris on the other hand had a sharp tongue, always smartly dressed and had an independent income, which enabled her to buy expensive gifts. She never had time for me. She never seemed to care about anyone else, but sought endless attention and admiration, tried to impress everyone she met and criticized everyone – family and friends. She took on every duty, other than physical, for her parents, especially their business and banking matters.

After fifteen months the country mansion at Wilbraham was taken over by the War Department and Elizabeth and I were moved back into the town, separately. A variety of billets followed. Mrs Jones' contribution to the War Effort was to house and feed an evacuee for one term. Though the Joneses spoke perfect English if they wished, they conversed solely in Welsh in front of me unless addressing me personally – which was very seldom. I spent lonely hours reading in bed, almost fully dressed against the cold, until Mrs Jones angrily accused me of wasting her 'electrics' and removed the only light bulb. Then there was Mrs Williams who was fifty-four inches round the waist and her grinning dentures masked a vile temper. The front parlour of her council house, used only for interviews with visiting school staff, was immaculate. The kitchen and scullery where we lived and ate, with a never-groomed long-haired cocker spaniel, was not. The only time I recall seeing the dustpan and brush in use was when our hostess swept up the contents of a paper bag of porridge oats which had burst onto the floor, the contents then tipped into another bag. We had grit and dog-hairs in our porridge daily for the next week! Fatty Williams disliked the other girl billeted there with me. Wanting to save trouble with extra laundry, Fatty decided we must both share her bed, and insisted I must be in the middle. But when Fatty saw Maureen scraping the mildew from under a slice of elderly homemade cake, she told the Billeting Officer to remove her (lucky Maureen). I remember Fatty complaining of itching and came home with a tin of ointment from her doctor. 'He's told me to spread it on all over, but I'm too big to reach, so you'll have to do it,' she told me. And began to strip off in front of the fire, for me to proceed, daily! I had never seen a grown-up naked before and this was not a good introduction.

When my Gran and Aunt Doris met me at Hereford railway station for the Christmas 1942 holidays, they were horrified. I was thin, yellow, with a row of five styes on one eye, and one on the other, plus a boil on the bridge of my nose and I was itching all over. They marched me straight to their doctor who diagnosed anaemia, head lice and scabies, prescribing Parishes Food (iron), solution for daily hair wash, Permanganate of Potash for daily baths and a tin of sulfur ointment (same as Fatty had). Extended daily bed rest, and clothes and bed linen to be changed daily. There was no question of me returning to Denbigh for the Spring Term. I was rather bored with the prospect; Auntie Doris, on whom the remedial work would fall, was horrified, and Gran relieved her fury on our Headmistress, Miss Ellershaw. However, at least I was with my family. Though of course there were arguments. Sometimes we were visited by friends, neighbours and even family who lived in the area; and invariably, when they smiled, shook hands or kissed and departed, Gran and Auntie would compete with their criticisms of them – with which I invariably, vehemently disagreed. Following which, much to my amusement, Gran would refuse to speak to me for two or three days!

Their apartment was on the first floor of a lovely house overlooking the River Wye, with the city and cathedral just on the other side, and lovely public parks all around. Sadly, they were not there for very long, with their constant criticisms causing friction with everyone. However, they were generally very kind to me; Dodo (as Auntie Doris had asked me to call her) loved to take me shopping when I needed clothes. She used my Clothes Ration Coupons and knowing my love of pony books and horses, bought me some lovely books. Later on she arranged riding sessions for me at stables nearby.

I was back in Denbigh for the Summer Term of 1944, and the D-Day landings! I had various stays at the hostel in Grove Road, between billets, but my last billet was the best, with 'Uncle Bob and Auntie Fan', a lovely couple, full of fun and laughter, who made me feel very welcome. Emotionally, there were two outstandingly bad times though. Birthdays had always been very special occasions in our family. Much ceremony had been observed over the opening of cards, giggles of suppressed excitement escaping at the unwrapping of weirdly shaped parcels. There were tea parties with candles and visitors arriving with hugs and kisses. In Denbigh, no one was aware it was my twelfth birthday, and I was shy to mention it as though prompting friends. I received not one single card, present or 'Happy Birthday' wish. I went to bed that night feeling quite numb.

Being an only child I had read a great deal before the war and a favourite set of books were my Golden Pathways with their myths and legends, Aesop's Fables, pictures and descriptions of the Seven Wonders of the World, of ancient Greece and Rome. When Miss Ellershaw asked us to write a description of an ancient city as seen in the first century AD for Scripture homework, I drew on my memory of those books for my essay. At our next Scripture lesson, having marked our books, she handed them out to each girl, reading out her marks and comments, leaving mine till last, unmarked, she explained, as I had obviously copied it. This I hotly denied and was promptly given a punishment for lying. Was she 'getting at me' because Gran had me removed from my first billet, and subsequently criticised the fact I was left in a dreadful billet till I was too ill to return to school for a whole term? I only know that it was the start of our mutual loathing, which continued when I reported the loss of my purse, containing twenty-one sixpenny pieces (ten shillings and sixpence) which I was saving up in hopes of buying myself a bicycle – and again was accused of lying. When the purse was eventually found and handed in to her, complete with the twenty-one sixpences, she never had the grace to apologise. And on my fifteenth birthday, just eight days after the liberation of Guernsey, when each from the very first huge batch of letters from home was handed out to the excited recipients, there was nothing for me. That is, until mine alone was handed to me by Miss Ellershaw after lunch. I remain convinced that she held it back deliberately, so as to inflict on me, hours of excruciating misery. But by this time, most ordinary hurts and disappointments hardly mattered: I had grown a tough shell. I was my own person, made my own decisions about clothes, hairstyles, the hours and company I kept. Some right, some undoubtedly wrong. But this independence sustained me during the hours, weeks, years of waiting for the ultimate goal: the return to the safety and comfort of my parents and my island home.

At six thirty on the morning of August 5th, the sun rose from behind Sark to blaze a golden path across the still glassy surface of the Little Russel, and St Peter Port, crowned by the Victoria and Elizabeth College towers, was bathed in a glorious pink haze. I had maintained a belief that Guernsey was lovely, but no childish memory could have prepared me for the fairytale beauty of that scene, as our ship rounded St Martin's Point and slid gently towards the harbour heads, her rails lined with the returning, exultant exiles. During the three intervening months since liberation, several photos had been enclosed

in my parent's letters, warning, if not fully preparing me for the sight of a gaunt, white-haired couple who had been my strong, athletic, sports-mad parents. And judging by their expressions of astonishment, they were equally unprepared for their daughter's return. Maybe they tried to mask their feelings, I don't know, but their dismay at that moment of realization that the little girl who was sent away five years ago in her gymslip, would never, ever return, was clearly visible to me.

There followed months of effort on both sides, interspersed with moments of fun and laughter, introspection and tears. I was a prematurely developed young adult, who had become mentally and physically independent through force of circumstance, now deeply resentful of the emotional demands and the newly imposed authority of my parents. I thought my little brother, born during the occupation, was adorable, but failed to understand why I should repeatedly be required to play nursemaid and babysitter at a moment's notice, regardless of any previous arrangements I might have made with friends. I had returned to the island confident and self-possessed, keen to show off to my parents my achievements in music, art and sport, the subjects in which they had particular

interest. But although they duly expressed appreciation, table talk was invariably dominated by the traumas and privations they had suffered, and their unending need for sympathy. Mutual love and understanding was missing: our loving relationship had been broken and apparently it was all my fault. The guilt was enormous.

Fifty years later, at the invitation of the then headmistress Mary Steel, twenty-nine of us 'girls' returned to Howells School for a reunion. A fabulous occasion in so many respects. We were royally entertained, not least at the marvelous dinner with the Howellian Alumni on the Saturday night – lovely food, lots of wine, speeches, laughter and tears – and then more wine! And that night in our dormitories, in our nighties and dressing gowns, with the help of wine-loosened tongues, we dared admit to each other for the first time, our personal feelings of guilt – that the loving relationship between ourselves and our parents, had never returned. It was an enormous relief to share our emotional loss. We had enjoyed our revisit to Denbigh, and several of us said how nice it would be to have lunch together one day. Which was such fun we have repeated our 'Denbigh Lunches' every month ever since. We also attend The Ladies' College Guild AGM every year. And recently, the College has expanded. We were invited, as a group, to see over the building extensions and, as a matter of interest, were asked which room we liked best. We chose a lovely conference room with an extensive view of the island. A few of us were invited back to a further viewing, and there, on the door of our chosen room, was a splendid notice: THE DENBIGH ROOM.

There are only six Denbigh Girls now surviving. We all arrived for our final monthly gathering this January, on one or two walking sticks or a Zimmer frame, complaining that we are forbidden wine with our various medications, laughing hilariously over our past and present experiences together.

Siân Jones

This digital print is taken from one of the original posters displayed at the Occupation Museum in Guernsey. These posters were authorised as an incentive planned by the States of Guernsey in order to distil the panic on the island at the time. Residents had to decide whether to leave their home and move to the UK or to remain on the island and face the prospect of German occupation.

The choice of words, however, are far from calm. The use of capital letters and exclamation marks makes this poster appear paradoxical, especially as some people only had twenty-four hours to make their decision.

'Untitled' uses distorted text which gives a sense of confusion, similar to the emotions that the islanders would have felt reading the original poster at that time.

'Untitled'
Siân Jones
Digital Print
42CM X 60CM

Margaret Le Conte

Taken from a conversation with Olympia and written as a monologue in Margaret's own words.

I was ten years old at the beginning of the war and fifteen-and-a-half when I came back. The end of the war was in May 1945 and we came back on the 19th of September, quite a while after. You see you had to wait your turn and you were notified when you could come back.

We were all over the place at the beginning of the occupation. Obviously you went with your school at ten years old. I went with Capelles School and we were some of the last children to leave. We waited from eight o'clock in the morning right through to about two the following morning before the bus came for us. Soon after that, my Mother left with my brother, David, who was three months old at the time. She left about half-past eleven that morning. Apparently they went to Bolton.

Capelles School was taken to Weymouth, and then there was the long train journey up to Wigan. *That* train journey! That's why I don't like travelling – it was the most horrendous journey that I've ever been on. Talk about a fairground ride adventure. I was terrified. All of the stations were blacked out. *Everything* was blacked out. We were travelling at night and we had all of the blinds down to make sure that there was no light coming through the windows. I was the oldest child with a lot of younger ones in my class and they were all terrified too. Most of us had never been on a train before, I had when I was two years old, but I couldn't remember what it was like. We didn't know the noises of the train and every time we went into a tunnel, every time we went through a railway station, the noises changed and we were all scared stiff. They had

removed all of the names from the railway stations too, so you couldn't tell where you were. I think we eventually went to sleep, I can't remember. But oh, we were so frightened, all the way up to Wigan from Weymouth.

When our school arrived in Wigan, I was billeted with a billeting officer. After a month they decided that Wigan wasn't safe, as it was too close to the Manchester bombings. So we were moved down to Nantwich. Unbeknown to me the billeting officer had found out where my mother was. So, after a month in Wigan, I then joined my mother in Bolton. She was with a very nice elderly couple who promised to take just one adult and one child. My brother was ill. He had pneumonia and spent the first four months in hospital. He nearly died at six months old and this was almost to the day that I lost my sister five years earlier to pneumonia. Poor mum had quite a time of it. When David eventually came out, we had to contact the authorities to find us new lodgings.

We ended up with another elderly couple, Mr and Mrs Owen. They had five sons and Mr Owen was very strict. One day when I was doing my homework, I couldn't draw a straight line and he got so furious at me. There was no sort of kindness there. Unfortunately, about a month after we'd moved in, Mrs Owen climbed up some steps to get something out of a cupboard, fell and broke her leg. Her sons all came back on compassionate leave, so we had to get out and they literally kicked us out onto the street!

We had nowhere to go, so the Minister of the nearby church took us in. It was supposed to be for three or four nights. We were on camp beds and mattresses on the floor in his study, but we ended up being there six weeks! Finally he found us two very nice ladies, Dorothy and her mother (I can't recall their surname). They took us in and they couldn't have been nicer. They were lovely to us and they weren't too far from the hospital either, which was good because my brother had to go for regular check ups.

The air in Bolton at that time was very smoky, due to all the mills. My brother was becoming ill again and the doctor said that we had to get out of that atmosphere. There was no way that he'd improve. He'd be ill every winter if he stayed there, in fact he could have died. My mother didn't know what to do but she had a sister, who was also evacuated with her children and was living in Eaton Bray, near Dunstable. It was a lovely little village with a village pond and a small school. There were only two classes and one of the teachers was a Jersey lady. If you wanted books, the library van came once a week. You also had to have your teeth seen to – they came to the school in a caravan. It was quite different there, and I had my three cousins, my auntie with her two girls and a boy and we all lived together in the same house.

My auntie had some friends that lived in the north and they wanted to come and see her. My mother had also heard from her friend Elsie Robilliard, to say that she had a friend that lived in Harpenden and this friend would love to see mum. This lady was a matron of a nursing home and Elsie asked if mum would like to go and see her. So, we said yes, and the Corbetts came down and took our bedroom while we went off to see her. But just as we got there, two of my cousins and one of the other children came down with scarlet fever. And of course my brother and I had been with them. In those days it was a very bad thing. The authorities came in wearing full body armour. They fumigated all of the rooms with smoke bombs and sealed them off. For many days we weren't allowed to go in. Fortunately my cousin Joan and I neither got it, nor did David. But they thought we might go down with it at any time, so David and I had to live in a tent in the garden for a week. Luckily it was the summer.

We were only supposed to be there for a couple of days, but because my mother had been a nurse back home in Guernsey, she offered to help. I looked after my brother and took him out for walks so that we didn't make any noise or disturb anyone. At the end of the week, they decided that they'd take us on for good – we could live there and my mother took on a full time nursing job. My brother and I slept in the nurses' quarters with my mother. We were all in the same room because there was just one room available. We ended up being there for four years.

Mum enrolled me into the local convent school, St Dominic's, and it was the best school that I'd ever been to. First of all, we were all girls. There were only twelve of us in the class, so we were all friends and I had a very close friend called Monica. It felt like I belonged and that was really lovely! The nuns were very good to me and in fact, from what I'd later heard, I went in at a lower fee than they normally charged (to help out my mother).

My brother went to a full-time nursery school which I passed on my way to school. So I used to take him there in the morning, go to school, pick him up at dinner time, take him home, bring him back again, and do the same in the evening. When we got home at the end of the day, I had to take him out for a walk for an hour or so and then give him his tea, bathe him, and put him to bed. Mum helped whenever she could, but I had the responsibility of doing it all, because Mum was working so hard. And then I did my homework afterwards – but these were good days.

We used to go to church every Sunday, and we had a really good Sunday School there. We would go to church in the morning and then Sunday School in the afternoon. Because I was one of the oldest children, I used to take the collection. When it came to the sermon during the service in the morning the children left, so I used to take my brother up as far as the common. There was a little sandpit there and we'd play for a little bit. Then after ten minutes or so, we'd walk back to the church. One day we were walking back and we heard a doodlebug over our heads. They made a very particular sound. When you

didn't hear it anymore, that meant that it was coming down. This one stopped right over our town. Well I don't think I've *ever* run so fast in my life and I really could run! I ran past all the shops with their big windows, mind you they were all taped up with parcel tape. But didn't I *run*! I had to pass a little road that went to the police station and there were two policemen shouting, 'Get into shelter!' I ran with David and the pushchair. When I arrived at the church, I saw that there were steps to get up into the church and I knew I wouldn't be able to get him up in time, so I ran round the corner to the Sunday School.

I was trying to open the door when the bomb landed.

I didn't have a chance to open the door to get into shelter, so I came round the front of the church again.

The doodlebug landed on the common, not very far from where we'd been playing, a bit further along by a potato patch. Three quarters of the common was planted up for potatoes, as they did in those days. My mother was in church at the time and the minister stopped his sermon and said 'We'll pray'. My mother knew we'd gone to the common and when she heard it go off in that direction, she came out as fast as she could. And there I was standing with my brother quietly waiting. My brother turned to me one day and said, 'Mother told me the story of the doodlebug,' and he said, 'Well I must thank you for not just leaving me and running for it!' I never thought of leaving him – it'd never crossed my mind.

My brother was never any trouble. He was only a year old at that time and my friend Monica had lost her father when she was two years old. Her mother was a housekeeper to two elderly gentlemen, so we had to be quiet around there too. We weren't allowed to play in the garden either, so she used to come out with me and David for a walk. We'd have a good old chat. We kept in touch for seventy years, right up until last year when she died.

My mother started packing the day the war ended! We applied to go home straight away. *Now we're going back!* I remember thinking. I'd been waiting for this moment for a long time. My dad had stayed behind. When we arrived back in Guernsey my brother, of course, never knew my father. He was only three months old when we'd left the island. Mother and I could see my father from the boat. We were waving and David said 'Which one's my dad?' My mother was saying 'The one with the brown hat'. He stared at every brown hat, searching for our dad. Oh yes, I recognised dad straight away. But I'd changed from a ten year old girl he'd known to a young lady of fifteen-and-a-half.

I remember that there were no cars to collect us from the harbour that day, so we had to walk from the White Rock in town all the way back to our home. My uncle had brought his bicycle for my brother to sit on. I remember carrying my bags and we put a suitcase on the back of the bicycle too. That was a long walk to Capelles that day.

My brother didn't know my father, and living in a nursing home meant that he'd always been around women. He'd never lived with a man and my father was very careful. He didn't push himself on him in any way. Perhaps his shoelace would come undone, my father would say 'I can do it up for you'.

'No my mummy will do it', he'd say. There was a lot of that. My father would say 'Yes, your mummy will do it for you, I'll tell her for you' and just left it at that. But then one day, my father was shaving and he'd left the bathroom door open. When my brother passed by he said, 'What are you doing to your face?' so my dad said 'Oh, I'm having a shave,' and he said 'Why?'. So my brother stayed out in the hall and my father just spoke to him and explained about it and he said 'When you're doing it again, will you let me know?' and every day my father would say 'I'm going to shave now David, do you want to come and see?' – he'd go and watch and they gradually got closer and closer.

I was happy to be home and my relationship with my dad was no different. I was still his scamp. His little girl that was always in trouble. He sent a lovely letter to Monica once, to say that it was nice that she'd been my friend during the war and that he remembers all the little antics I used to get up to and that he'd hoped that I'd grown out of a lot of them – and that he was very grateful to her, but he thought it was his turn to have me now. It was a lovely little letter. A few years ago her family sent it to me as a keepsake. I have it with me now. It reminds me of her and my dad.

Molly Harris

Coastal Defence

For centuries the population of Guernsey had to defend their island by building **Coastal Defences**. To this day examples remain of Martello towers, forts, bunkers, gun emplacements and anti-tank beach defences.

'Coastal Defence'
Molly Harris
Acrylic
22CM X 20CM

Janet de Santos

My mother Elisabet Fink was born in Vienna on 21 July 1909 – although the German authorities in occupied Guernsey record her date of birth as 1899. Her brother Johan Fink was born in Vienna in May 1911. Their parents were Samuel Fink, born in Vienna in 1882, and Fanny Grosz, born 1893, whose place of birth is recorded variously as Poland or Czechoslovakia. My Christian name was chosen in memory of my maternal grandmother Jeanette Grosz.

The family lived in an apartment near the Vienna Opera house and music played a big part in their life. My uncle known as Hans played the violin and my mother known as Liesl played the piano and sang. My grandfather had stables in Vienna and was a horse dealer, while my grandmother travelled extensively in Europe dealing in antique paintings and carpets, often accompanied by her son Hans.

They were part of a large Jewish community in Vienna, 200,000 of whom fled the Nazis or died in concentration camps when the Germans annexed Austria on March 13, 1938. My grandfather died in Buchenwald. My grandmother escaped to Prague, moved to Brussels and subsequently went by sea to São Paolo, Brazil where she died aged 51 in 1944. Her son Hans joined the volunteer Czech army in Prague and managed to reach England in 1942 with the remnants of the Czech army and was stationed in Warwickshire.

My mother Liesl came to Guernsey on October 23, 1937. A friend of my mother August Spitz (Gusti) had arrived in September 1937 and they were joined by a third Viennese Jew Teresa Steiner in 1939. I have various photos of my

mother and Gusti at this period and also a photo which appears to have been sent to her brother from Guernsey in 1939. I have learnt from David Le Cheminant, a retired Guernsey vet, that my mother worked for his parents Norman and Ethel Le Cheminant, owners of a toy shop in St Peter Port, at their bungalow in Cobo and was still with them when he was evacuated from the island with Elizabeth College.

My father's family were well-known in the Cobo area. My grandfather Henry Thomas Duquemin was a grower and exporter of tomatoes and flowers, while my grandmother

34

had also established a business at Cobo Post Office which included, in addition to the post office, a general stores, milk round, tearoom and shooting range. Their eldest son Harry, my father was the postmaster and general manager. My father had been left a widower when his first wife tragically died at an early age, and I am told by relatives that the Duquemin family were delighted when he met and married my mother. The marriage took place on February 12, 1940 at St Sampson's Church. I have a somewhat tattered photocopy of the report of the event which appeared in the local paper. My father's sister and brother-in-law ran an hotel at Les Pieux, Cobo and it was here that the reception took place. Gusti Spitz was chief bridesmaid and other Austrian friends were invited and appear in various photos. In addition, according to the press report, my mother's own mother had been informed of the wedding because she managed to send flowers from Belgium.

My parents began their married life living at Cobo Post Office which had a pleasant residential wing, with lovely views towards Grandes Rocques from the first floor rooms. However, by the summer of 1940, Guernsey had ceased to be the safe haven to which the Austrian women had fled. The UK decided not to defend the islands against the Germans who had by now reached the French channel coast and on June 29, 1940 the German occupation began.

In October 1940 Jews were required to register with the Guernsey Police and as a result in November 1940 names of five foreign women were passed to the German authorities – my mother being one of them. Having witnessed at first-hand discrimination against the Jewish population in Germany and Austria during the 1930s, the Austrian Jews would have had no illusions about the significance of this act – even if some Guernsey people in places of authority appeared somewhat cavalier with regard to the probable consequences of the information

provided by them. Nevertheless, the next eighteen months or so appear to have passed with a certain degree of normality. My father continued to run the Post Office and my mother became pregnant. Germans were billeted at Les Pieux Hotel, but according to my cousin who was a teenager at the time, the first soldiers there were mainly well-educated English speakers who behaved well. Later in the occupation, my aunt and uncle were less fortunate with their 'guests'.

I was born in July 1941 at the Castel Hospital where both Gusti Spitz and Teresa Steiner worked. Gusti was a very frequent visitor to Cobo and was very well-liked by all the Duquemin clan there. By March 1942, however, a curfew of 8pm-6am had been imposed on the Jews and they had to remain at their current addresses. Non-compliance would result in a fine, imprisonment or internment in a camp for Jews. Shortly after, in April 1942, my parents were visited by Gusti and Teresa. The two women had been told that they were being deported with immediate effect and were apparently absolutely terrified. My father often spoke with great sadness of this last visit when he lent Gusti a suitcase – fearing no doubt that this farewell might be a final one. As indeed it was. Both women were to die in Auschwitz.

It is assumed that my mother avoided deportation at this stage because she had British nationality through marriage. However, the event underlined the precariousness of her position. In May 1942 there is a German reference to my father being the husband of a Jew and the owner of a shop. This is followed in June by the order that Jews are to wear the Star of David. In August 1942 Jews are banned from places of public entertainment and may shop only between 3-4pm.

In September 1942 came the first mass deportation to Germany of non-island-born persons. My mother was not included in this group but a German letter dated January

5th, 1943 indicates that the deportation of Jews was now in sight. Notices for departure were in fact issued on February 3rd, 1943. Those involved were listed as Jews, leading freemasons, officers, public figures, wealthy individuals, Sarkese and undesirables. My father always joked that he must have belonged to the final group. My father had actually appealed by letter against the deportation order. But to no avail – friends of his have, however, told me that he could have remained in Guernsey, but very much in character, he opted to go as a family group.

The original departure date advised was February 9th, but my parents and I actually left the island on February 12th. I was told later that we travelled in a force ten gale in the hold of a filthy coal ship. The only luggage allowed was what one could carry. Packing for three people, including a baby of eighteen months must have been difficult! My mother was terribly ill and for the rest of her life found it very difficult to board a ship, even in the calmest of harbours. Once we arrived in St Malo, we were put on a train and remained locked in for several hours despite local air raids. Apparently, I ended up in my carrycot under the carriage seat for protection.

It must have been a terrible blow for my parents when they were split up. I am sure that the hope had been that as a family unit we would have been sent to the CI family camp at Biberach. In the event, my father was sent to Laufen in Germany, the camp for single men and my mother and I were sent to Compiègne in France. I have read Nellie Le Feuvre's account of her time in Compiègne and it certainly matches the impression of dirt and degradation given me by my mother. While there, much to my mother's horror, I became infested with lice and had to have all my hair cut off. The worst aspect of Compiègne, however, was the fact that my mother was appointed barrack leader – possibly because she was bilingual in German and English. This meant that she was very much in the spotlight where the Germans were concerned. Her papers identified her as Jewish and in the next-door camp people were being loaded onto transport and taken off to concentration camps. As a result, it must have come as an enormous relief when we left Compiègne in June 1943 and were transported to Biberach. My father, in his turn, was transferred to Biberach in August 1943.

By the time we all arrived in Biberach, camp conditions there were reasonably comfortable, especially when compared to Compiègne. Even more important, I am sure, was the fact that we were a family unit again, which must have been a great help to my mother and the whole point of my father opting not to stay behind in Guernsey. Although in the same camp, men lived separately from the women and children and my mother and I shared a room with Mrs Bertram Bartlett and her son Robin, who had also been transferred from Compiègne. My father helped in the camp kitchens – principally peeling potatoes! Although only three years old, I was allowed to attend the infant school and had many other children to play with. I am sure that life was not as carefree for my parents, but finally, on April 23, 1945, the camp was liberated by the Free French. Four weeks later we were taken to a US airforce base and flown by Dakota to Hendon in the UK. Once we had been processed, we went to Paignton in Devon where my grandmother's brother, Albert Guilbert, had settled after his retirement from the navy.

I am not sure how long we stayed in Paignton, but we were definitely back living at Cobo Post Office in December 1945, when my mother's brother travelled from England to stay with us for Christmas. They had last seen one another in Austria in 1937 and in the intervening period had lost both their parents and nearly all of their immediate family. To my knowledge only three family members survived the German occupation of Europe – two were allowed to settle in America after their liberation from concentration camps and one settled in Brussels.

My uncle settled in Warwickshire and achieved British nationality in 1948. Over time he was able to establish his own business and in the immediate postwar years was greatly helped by the cooperation and assistance of the many Jewish refugees in the UK. There was virtually a Jewish colony of displaced persons in one street of Leamington Spa where he lived.

My mother, on the other hand, continued to live in the totally non-Jewish environment of Guernsey. She no longer had her friend Gusti and now knew that her family was gone and her old life in Vienna had been obliterated forever. She visited Vienna only once in the postwar years and never wanted to go again. She was even reluctant to play the piano any more – although she was very gifted.

Even when her brother bought her a piano as a gift, it was difficult to persuade her to play.

Gradually, however, she settled back into family life in Guernsey. Her cooking became part of local folklore – especially her *apfelstrudel* and *wiener schnitzel*. She also became something of an entrepreneur, setting up a very successful guest house on the coast road at Cobo.

She finally left the island when my father died in 1970 and bought an apartment in Spain, where I was then living. When I returned to the UK to help my uncle with his businesses in Warwickshire, my mother also decided to come back to the UK and, as a result, her final years were spent in Leamington Spa.

Molly Harris

Boundary

This painting depicts barbed wire, which was the boundary of choice by the occupying forces during the war. Over forty percent of the island's population was evacuated to the mainland, and the twenty thousand people who chose to remain were subjected to curfews and restrictions enforced by these violent boundaries.

'Boundary'
Molly Harris
Acrylic
31CM X 45CM
(By kind permission of
Rodney & Elmarie Brache)

Ethel Brouard

A Child Apart

I am the eldest of three children born to Cecil Ernest and Reta Mary Le Noury of the Castel Parish. They were young, hard-working growers and owned their own small vinery growing tomatoes and flowers. In June 1940 the tomato crop was at its peak and it was very hard for them to leave the island suddenly, shutting the doors on the greenhouses and their crops. When the opportunity came for their school-age children to leave the island for their own safety, they reluctantly agreed, thinking it would be for a period of weeks. Little did they realise it would be five years before they would see each other again.

In my memory, it was a lovely, warm June day – and in fact my father's birthday. The school must have been closed because of the emergency, but I remember playing on Cobo Beach with other children when an older girl came running up to us and told us to go home immediately as we were to go to England the next day. I do not remember having any knowledge of the potential invasion by the Germans and just felt excitement at what was going to happen. My younger brother, Raymond, and myself were to go to the school the following day to travel to England with the school, accompanied by teachers and some mothers as helpers. We could only take luggage that we could carry, so two small suitcases were hurriedly packed and food had to be taken for the journey.

Not many memories remain about our travels, except much waiting around in church halls and sleeping on floors. Long train journeys with tired fractious children and eventually arriving in Bury, a town on the outskirts of Manchester. We stayed in Bury for about two weeks.

We were placed in council houses, one teacher to ten children. I can remember sharing beds top and tail and living on sliced bread and cheap jam. (Sliced bread was a great novelty as I had never seen this before.) A mobile soup kitchen came around the houses but we did not like the food offered and preferred our jam sandwiches.

We spent the days playing in fields behind the houses but the problem was that we had few clothes with us. In her hurry, my mother had packed our 'best' clothes and we had no other play clothes. Local people came to the rescue and we received the first of many donations. Kindly local people befriended us and I remember being invited to tea with a very genteel elderly lady, which must have been a strange experience for her. Apparently, the local people did not expect that we would speak the English language and knew very little about the Channel Islands.

From Bury, the Castel School travelled to Cheshire, and the school was divided between three villages, Ollerton, Warburton and Pickmere. Raymond went to Warburton and I found myself in a large hall in Pickmere. Local people were taking children home with them and the rest of us were 'scooped up' by a large, friendly lady and taken back to her farmhouse. Soon most of the children had been found homes and I stayed with her, Mrs Evelyn Platt, together with one schoolteacher, Miss Phyllis Ninnim. Eventually, my brother arrived from Warburton, as it was a policy to keep brothers and sisters together.

Mr Arthur Platt and his wife Evelyn lived in a rambling farmhouse in a state of great discord. Apparently they disliked each other intensely and I never saw them sit and eat at the same table. As small children, we were not at first aware of this but soon accepted the situation. Mrs Platt was a large, good-humoured lady, generous and kind. We were immediately taken to Knutsford to buy essential clothes and a large bar of Terry's chocolate. Mr Platt was a cattle dealer and frequently travelled to Ireland buying cows, which would arrive at Lostock station and would have to be collected by a farmhand and anyone who could be roped in to help. Life at Mere View Farm was very different to any life we had known in Guernsey.

Everyone was expected to do their share of work, not least the children. My brother and I were often expected to do the washing up and serve milk at the door. My brother helped with herding cows and was often expected to go to the station with the farmhand to collect the cows. I remember being told that he had been seen crying in the middle of the road because the cows were going in different directions and he did not know what to do. He

must have been only about eight years old at the time. Mrs Platt was financially independent of her husband, which I understand was one cause of the trouble between them, as she refused him control of her money. They each had a small car, which were used when petrol was available, but Mrs Platt had a heart condition and liked my brother to accompany her on any car trip so that he could put the brake on if she felt ill!! Mr Platt, or Father Platt, as he was generally called by his wife, was a 'brooding presence'. He was a sandy-haired, red-faced angry-looking man, or so it seemed to me as a child. I cannot remember ever having a conversation with him. He appeared to spend most of his time in a little wooden office attached to one of the barns and only came into the house for meals and to sleep. I was sometimes sent to knock on the door of the office to ask him for eggs, preserved in a 'water-glass' solution, which were kept in his office – a strange place to keep the eggs! I think I was generally rather frightened of him, especially after one incident when he had used a favourite silver teapot belonging to his wife and damaged it. Obviously they had strong words about this and he came back into the house with his gun under his arm and said he would 'put a bullet through the teapot and in everyone else as well'.

Much of our time at the appropriate season was taken up by picking the fruits of the garden. A large garden at the front of the house was planted with black and red currants, raspberries and rhubarb. We were expected to help with this and the jam making. I don't remember how Mrs Platt obtained the sugar, as it was severely rationed at the time, but I discovered later that she shopped in a small grocery shop in a very run-down area of Northwich. Many families could not afford their rations and it appeared she was able to buy extra. Mrs Platt cooked huge dinners with lots of puddings and cakes. We were always extremely well fed.

The farm kitchen was very big. A full-size billiard table filled the space in the middle, covered in a checked oil baize. All the life of the kitchen took place around this table. I never saw it used for billiards or uncovered for that matter. During air raids we slept under it, protected from the cold by large sheets of cardboard all around. An old-fashioned coal range was used for cooking, augmented by an electric cooker. There was a grandfather clock in one corner of the kitchen and another table by a window, at which Mr Platt sat to eat. He never ate in the dining room with us. Adjoining the kitchen was a very large, walk-in larder with large shallow pans containing milk which was left to settle for butter and cream.

After a few months, life at the farm seemed quite normal. We never knew what to expect. We could come home from school to find that we would all pile into the car to go to the cinema in Northwich. Mrs Platt liked to see the newsreels and we always seemed to be included in these outings, we even had a visit to Manchester to see a pantomime once.

Manchester was experiencing bombing raids during that first year and a bomb shelter had been dug out in the garden. It was lined with corrugated iron and it was dripping wet. We only went in it once. Everyone hated the shelter. Fortunately, Pickmere only experienced a few bombs, mainly it seems from German planes jettisoning their bombs. One night we had many incendiary bombs dropped on the village but very little damage occurred. However, the nights could be noisy and disturbed by the extensive bombing of nearby Manchester.

The Guernsey children billeted in the village of Pickmere were to attend a small church school in the village of Wincham and I can remember arriving at this large oak door which was opened by a teacher dressed in a flowered overall who was the sole teacher at this small school. The school now had three teachers, Miss Ninnim and Miss Duchemin from Guernsey and Miss Molly Cawley. The children seemed to integrate into the life of the school with no problems – dinners were eaten at the school, cooked by one of the local mothers. An air raid shelter was built in the playground and we carried our gas masks at all times. Clothing was often a problem for us. We received coats from Canada at one time, all the same style but different colours. We were given old hand-knitted jumpers which we unravelled and I learnt to knit myself 'new' jumpers and every Sunday afternoon I had to darn my own socks for the next week!

I must now speak of Miss Phyllis Ninnim, the schoolteacher billeted with us. I owe her an immense debt of gratitude. Without her, our life would often have been difficult in that strange household. She was fun, treated us with affection and was always there for us. She really was our substitute mother. She bought us Christmas and birthday presents and much-needed clothes with the very limited money she was earning. I remember her with great affection. Miss Ninnim, or Aunty Phyl, as we later called her, was a remarkable woman and a role model for me in later life.

My life continued in this vein for about two years, when I took an examination to ascertain if I had reached the educational standard necessary to transfer to one of the Guernsey Secondary Schools, the Ladies' College in Denbigh or the Intermediate School in Rochdale. I was accepted at the Ladies' College and moved to Denbigh in North Wales. My brother stayed on at Mere View Farm until he too moved to the Intermediate School in Oldham at nine years of age. Miss Ninnim had apparently written to the Guernsey Educational Authority in England saying that his education was suffering at this little church school as she felt he was very intelligent and would not achieve his potential there. It was agreed that he would go to Oldham.

I have no recollection of how I travelled to Denbigh. I assume I was accompanied to Chester and then travelled by train. My cousin, Ruth Gaudion, had evacuated with the Ladies' College and was then about 15 years old. She was billeted with a Mr and Mrs Percy Lewis in a small cottage on the slope of Denbigh Castle and they had kindly invited me to join her at their home. This home could not have been more of a contrast to Mere View Farm. This four-roomed cottage, rather grandly named Llwyfo House, was reached by a small, hilly path to the castle. The door led into a small sitting room but all the life of the house took place in a small living room with a black range with a clothes-draped fireguard in front The kitchen at the back was small, cheerless and dark with an old stone sink and a gas cooker. The lavatory was in a yard at the back. Mr and Mrs Lewis were kind and welcoming and my cousin was a familiar face. Denbigh was a small North Wales market town and lay in a valley between two low mountain ranges and was itself built on a small hill below a ruined castle. The Ladies' College had been billeted on a prosperous boarding school, Howell's School and had been allocated three of four classrooms and the use of the Lecture Theatre as a hall. Again, I soon settled into the life of the school. The girls were billeted with families in the town, some more happily than others. I think that during the war it was a rule that if a family had no children the wife was expected to do war work of some kind or take in evacuees. The Government allowance for an evacuee was 10/6 a week, if my memory serves me right. This was collected from the Post Office and must have been a bare minimum to provide food and shelter for a child for one week. Because of our home circumstances and the difficulty of doing homework in some of these homes, we were expected to go back to school for two hours during the evening. The teachers, almost without exception, were kind and dedicated and our welfare took up much of their time. Clothes and shoes were often a problem for the girls and again we had shoes and clothes donated from various sources.

We had much freedom on weekends and, if money permitted, would go to Rhyl by train, about 12 miles away,

to go to the cinema or walk along the promenade. Most of the amenities were closed for the duration of the war but some cafes were open and it seemed exciting to get on a train and see another town. At that time I was probably 12 years old and we seemed to be able to roam around at will and never felt in any danger. The countryside around Denbigh was very beautiful with small streams and woods – we walked and occasionally were taken to the moors where we picked bilberries. Girls at the Ladies' College with parents still in Guernsey were befriended by some local people and provided with pocket money. Miss Nancy Robinson, the sister of the headmistress of Howell's School, was my befriender and I think gave me sixpence a week pocket money and a prayer book on my confirmation.

School holidays were a problem for the children with no parents, or maybe just their mother, somewhere in England. Many of the mothers who had evacuated without their husbands had found employment as housekeepers and had no accommodation for their children. I had three uncles who had evacuated with their families but who lived some distance away. I was expected to write to them at the end of the term to ask them for the fare money and, with hindsight, this may have been one more problem for them. However, they always made me very welcome and provided a happy, friendly holiday home for me. One of my uncles lived in Peterborough and one in Doncaster. To travel to Peterborough I had to train to Chester, from there to Reading and then on to Peterborough. I would start early in the morning and arrive late in the afternoon. All this from the age of 11 years and totally alone.

My uncle in Doncaster was manager of a small, mixed nursery, growing various salad crops for the owner, a prosperous salesman in Doncaster market. Tomatoes and other vegetables were sold at the door and there were opportunities for me to earn pocket money. This was most welcome and I would at least go back to school with money for the term. I still had a lot of clothes given to me. I remember some kindly person bought me a new brown overcoat, which had been bought to last as it nearly dragged on the floor! My aunt was horrified when she saw this bedraggled child arrive and she found another coat for me, given by the sister of her employer. My uncle and aunt had two small children of their own and money was obviously scarce, but I was welcomed into their home and became very fond of them all.

On arrival again from a school holiday, Ruth and I found ourselves in another billet, with a Mr and Mrs Wainwright, an elderly couple who managed to run a very old Austin 7 car, in which they took us for expeditions (if they could scrounge enough petrol). Ruth and I were wedged into the back of this very small car, a food tin at our feet. This car had yellowing perspex windows – so that it always seemed to be a sunny day, whatever the weather! We were expected to make up a four at cards every evening, after which Mr Wainwright went to the pub for his nightly drink. They treated us very kindly and we stayed there until our return to Guernsey.

Strangely, I remember very little of our journey back to Guernsey. One of my first memories is walking along the harbour as our parents were not allowed there and had to wait for us at the Clock Tower. I can remember feeling very anxious and worried. I had become accustomed to my life in England, my comparative freedom and my independence and I did not really want to come back! My life had changed so much, I did remember what my parents looked like, but nothing of them as people. We were expected to go home with our relatively unknown parents and take up our lives, almost as if nothing had happened. I know I caused great hurt to my mother because she attempted to kiss me goodnight and I shrugged her off. I'd had very little physical affection in my later years and had been actively discouraged by a school friend from kissing anyone, having been told this was not done! My parents still remembered Ray and me as small children and we in no way resembled the children they remembered. Ray spoke with a broad Lancashire accent and I was tall and almost an adult. They had no idea of the life we had led.

Life became very difficult for us all. My youngest brother was six years old and suddenly had to get used to an older brother and sister. He had naturally been very indulged and we were entering a small, contained family unit. We felt like outsiders. My mother, in particular, could not cope with the situation. She had never travelled away from home on her own, had stayed at home with her family until she married, and did not understand us at all. The feelings were mutual. To give her credit, and with more understanding of the situation as I have got older, I think she tried hard but attempted to impose her will with petty rules, which we fought against and the situation did not improve. We both were unhappier than at any time during our time in England. She discouraged us from contacting our uncles because she felt that we were closer to them, which of course was true. My father, although more understanding, did not know what to do and the household was in turmoil.

I realise now that one would need to have been very wise and understanding to cope with such a situation. We were obviously 'street-wise' children, probably not very easy to handle and in no way prepared to accept the restrictions she tried to impose. We felt 'owned' and expected to love them immediately, and this could not be possible. The people we had been billeted with did not expect anything from us, except reasonable polite behaviour – there had not been any real closeness. The feeling of expectation from my mother was that we were happy to be home and would be happy ever after. This was an impossible dream and would come with time, if at all. The situation did not improve. I found my mother so impossible that I kept out of her way as much as possible. I now realise she too must have found her life very difficult with these awkward children suddenly in her life again.

The result was that Ray left home as soon as he conveniently could and I married and left home with great relief. When I look back on my childhood and my years in England and Wales, I feel I had gained from these experiences. I'd become self-reliant and self-confident. My younger brother, John, also felt somewhat apart from his brother and sister, although we did become much closer in later years. Ray and I tried to treat our mother with care and respect in her old age, but too many things had happened and too many harsh words spoken. Children taken from their parents at a youthful age cannot be assimilated into the family after a period of years without considerable trauma. This story was multiplied many times. This has only come to light in recent years when many of us spoke honestly about our problems. We were not able to do this while our parents were alive, as we did not want to cause them further hurt. The breaking of the family bond was such a loss to us all.

Olympia McEwan

Our lives in 25 words

This is a portrait of Olympia's step-father Edward 'Ted' Smith. Ted's father, Edward, remained in Guernsey during the occupation, while his mother, Blanche, evacuated to Nottingham with Ted, his brother Tony and other family members.

In her artwork, Olympia used copies of Red Cross letters that were sent between the couple to highlight the valuable service that the Red Cross administered during the German Occupation of the Channel Islands.

Red Cross letters were censored so that very little news could be communicated, and they were restricted to twenty-five words. Up to two letters could be sent or received per year, and they were the only means of contact that individuals could have with their loved ones.

These letters are a precious reminder of difficult times lived in adversity and the stoic nature of this special generation.

'Our lives in 25 words'
Olympia McEwan
Mixed media
127CM X 61CM

Trudie Shannon

Her Memory

She was twelve.
She and her mum had boarded the boat together.
Dad had said he'd meet them there.
He'd said, you go on ahead, I'll catch up.
But, he hadn't come, he'd had no intention of leaving.
And the gangway was pulled onboard without him.
She leaned on the rail,
Scanned all those faces, searching for his familiar one
But he wasn't there.
And the ship steamed away.
On the mainland, she went one way and her mum another.
She went on with the school
One of many farmed out, kid evacuees.
She vividly remembered her first night at their house.
Her pretending to be asleep whilst they unpacked her little case.
She remembered Aunty's comments
As she lifted aloft a pretty little camisole and matching pants
She can't be from a poor family, look at these.
And she had peeked a one eyed peek then
And wondered, how such lovely things came to be inside her case?
She had called them Aunty and Uncle
Though they would have preferred mum and dad
But she refused, she had a mum and dad.
Her dad alone in Guernsey guarding hearth and home.
Her mum working in the town earning pennies to survive.
But then The Hood was blown to smithereens
And her brother was killed, just nineteen
Her mum wanted her then, wanted a child by her side
So she sent for her
And she waved goodbye forever to
Aunty and Uncle who had been very kind.

She was nineteen when they came home together
Her grieving mother whose skin wept the tears she could not shed.
Dad was there to meet them off the boat.
He said their home was still there,
Though much of their furniture, their possessions had been destroyed.
He'd done his best, her grieving dad
Her thinner, greyer dad
But her dad, her dad,
Her dad was alive.
And the war was over, over
And she was no longer a child.

Jeni Snell

Screaming

Jeni Snell's art is based on the ongoing relationship she has with the place in which she grew up. Exploring her experience of living in a previously-occupied Channel Island, she is interested in the influence that our early environment has upon the formation of identity, especially in the LGBTIQA context, which she occupies.

Attending a school built on top of a WW2 German gun battery brought together the opposing dynamics of 'childhood innocence' and 'the architecture of war' within the playground and this conflicting and troubling relationship has been a consistently-developed theme throughout her work.

Using found objects, Jeni pays homage to Guernsey's significant WW2 legacy. She contextualises the islanders' make-do-and-mend creative resourcefulness whilst under occupation. A stark contrast to our current throwaway and materialistic global society malaise.

'Screaming'
Jeni Snell
acrylic and household paint on canvas
97CM X 97CM

Richard Fleming

Evacuation

The dog knows that there's something wrong:
he whines and scratches at the door.
My father says I must be strong,
there'll be new things and friends galore.
My mother folds and packs my frock,
white socks and underwear to change.
I hear the loud tick of the clock
and think that time is very strange:
it hurries on while we stand still
and never falters, never stops,
cares not for us and never will.
Mum packs a bag of lemon-drops.
I clutch Colette, my knitted doll.
My father lights a cigarette.
The clock still ticks down in the hall.
Poor Gran'mère seems to be upset.
The Ozannes' car stands at the gate.
Red-eyed, Mum hugs me, holds me tight.
Be quick, she says, they will not wait.
Says, promise me that you will write.
Dad says it's only for a while
There's sadness in my father's smile.

Shirley Falla

Taken from a conversation with Olympia and written as a monologue in Shirley's own words.

My very earliest memory is from 28th June 1940, I was with my grandma walking along the South Esplanade, where the Bus Terminus is now. We were walking along the path when suddenly my grandma pushed me and my lovely big doll, Phyllis, to the ground. Bombs were being dropped on the harbour. The Germans were bombing the tomato lorries, thinking they were carrying munitions. The tomato lorries were waiting there at the White Rock, for their boxes of tomatoes to be loaded onto cargo boats. My grandma held us both there and was covering us for protection. And that was the first thing that I remember as a child. I was two years old, and it still remains clear in my mind.

I also recall when the sirens used to go off, where we lived on Saints Road in the States' houses. When they went off, my brother and I were told to take shelter. So he went under his little desk and Mum and I used to go underneath the dining room table. We used to wait there until the sirens stopped and we were given the all clear. Afterwards my brother used to go outside with the rest of the boys on the estate, and these little three and four year-olds used to go and pick up pieces of shrapnel (which were still quite warm) which they'd collected and swap between them. I remember some of them were quite big pieces that dropped down on the estate. All through the war there were the sirens going off and we used to have to go for cover – but what sort of cover we had underneath a table, I don't know!

When the war started we lived at Moulin Huet in St Martins and my mum's family lived opposite Belgrave beach, nearly four miles away. Every day in the summer she used to walk us all down there, as it was one beach that was safe, and we could all be together as a family (most of the other bays on the island were mined). She was only twenty years old when the war started and we all had plenty of energy! I can remember she used to make my dad's dinner, she'd put his plate on a saucepan of hot water and leave it there for him for when he got home (in those days they used to have their main meal at lunchtime).

My father worked in greenhouses with his uncle who was like a father to him, and was the foreman of a vinery down at Petit Bôt. Well my dad used to have several little plots of land, about four or five, and he used to grow potatoes. When everything was being rationed, he used to hide them all in our bath – so we never had a bath during the whole of the occupation. Only tin baths for us in front of the fire!

I remember one day the cat caught a rabbit and brought it into the house. My Dad took it off the poor cat, cut the rabbit's head off, gave the head to the cat and we had the rest. That was a big treat for us. My Mum was incredibly brave. After curfew nobody was allowed out, but she used to go on her bike and cycle from Saints Road to Icart. There was a farmer who used to give her extra milk, because I never drank my milk ration at school – I hated it. So she used to make us a pink blancmange from the milk and carrageen moss, a seaweed which was dried and used as a jelly substitute. I remember we had nothing else, just this blancmange jelly for our tea every day. It was free and I loved it. (There would have been serious problems if she'd been caught though.)

I can remember clearly, my grandma used to give my brother and I a plate of winkles. She'd get the winkles off the beach and then boil them up, she'd hand us a darning needle each and we'd poke out the sea snail from the winkle and eat them. That was a big treat for us too! My Grandma would also have a square of chocolate for us and

we'd grate this square of chocolate on to a piece of bread. That was the chocolate that my grandpa had stolen! He worked at the White Rock and he used to steal it from the Germans. He also used to steal flour and my gran would make parsnip cake. She was very proud of her parsnip cake. She even said when the war was over, 'I'm still going to make my parsnip cake', but she never did. There was also my other gran and I remember going to see her once and they were eating potato peelings fried in linseed oil – which must have been absolutely horrible. People had to make do with whatever they could.

Unfortunately, my grandpa was eventually caught stealing. They searched the house and found that he had a radio too. So he was in big trouble and they sent him to prison. This was just before the end of the war. So on Liberation Day we were all standing outside the prison waiting for him to be released and he never was. So he wasn't able to join in the celebrations. My gran was in tears outside. That was really sad for us as a family.

I did go to school during the war. I went to Blanchelande when I was five, mid-way through the occupation. My brother went as well, towards the end of the war, and I can remember I used to have a little three-wheeler bike. My brother used to stand on the back and I would pedal us all the way down to school. There were about fifteen children and a couple of nuns. We had to learn a bit of German, which was expected of all school children at the time, but it was a way of life and we knew no different. We used to watch the Germans marching to music. We knew all the songs and we'd walk alongside them.

But my parents never ever had anything to do with the Germans, like a lot of people, they weren't going to associate with them. We didn't have any billeted with us, but my gran did. She had, not Germans, but French ladies that were brought over for the brothels. We weren't allowed to speak to them. I remember one of the French women wanted to put some perfume on me, and I can remember my gran saying 'No!' – we just weren't allowed to keep company with them.

One very sad story is about my uncle's wife. He was my gran's son (my mother's brother) and he'd joined the forces. He left his wife here and she stayed with my gran and grandpa. Unfortunately she started going out with some Germans. So she had to leave gran and grandpa's house – because that was absolutely a dreadful thing to do to her husband. He was in the Navy fighting the Germans and she was at home fraternising with them. She ended up having a German baby and at the end of the war she left the island. She did come back on holidays during the summer, but my mum and dad totally shunned her. They never had time for her.

One funny incident I remember was when my mum was pushing my brother in his pram. My grandpa had a big collection of smoking pipes on a pipe rack and my brother loved playing with them. So one day he gave my brother a pipe and there he was, sitting in his pram with this pipe poking out of his mouth. We were going on a walk up to the Bordage and you should have seen this German's face! He was highly amused and was wanting to stop and chat, and of course the last thing my mum wanted was having a German walking alongside. Anybody seeing would have thought she was fraternising and she was muttering under her breath to my brother, 'Don't, don't, don't – stop smiling at the German' and she thought in hindsight, this poor man probably had a little boy the same age. But you never knew which Germans were the awful ones. So there was no chit-chat for him that day. Not with us.

My father's boss used to give all the men vegetable soup to take home. We didn't need it, so my dad used to give it to the lady who lived next door who had a couple of children. She lived on her own and was in need of extra rations. But I always remember there came a time when we did need the soup and he was very upset when he had to tell her that he needed it for us. How on earth she managed after that I don't know. After the occupation there was a picture of my dad shaking hands with someone he knew, one of the soldiers, and his face was absolutely gaunt. He had lost so much weight.

One vivid memory I do have, is that somebody had drawn a V sign on the wall in St Martins, the V for Victory, and all the men in the parish had to do sentry duty at the Forest cemetery as punishment. They had to do it for several hours at a time and I know my dad had to relieve someone at three o'clock in the morning. Nobody was obviously going to admit to it and nobody would have wanted them to admit to it either.

When the occupation was over, I can remember my mum and dad saying to us, 'Come on, come on, let's all go down into town on the bikes!' Well, my mum and dad were on their bikes, with us on the back and we were covered in red, white and blue ribbons. You should have seen their bikes though! They had no tyres, they didn't have anything to repair them with, so they just used old hose pipes. We all went down into town and I can remember being at the White Hart watching all the soldiers passing by and, oh – it was wonderful, for everyone! We then somehow found our way to the Channel Islands Hotel and the soldiers were there on the steps – and they were throwing sweets down to us! I'll always remember trying to catch those sweets.

Paul Chambers

Molly Bihet

Storytelling has earned its place as the most important tradition humans possess. The reason for this being that every story contains a lesson to guide its audience.

Molly is our narrative; our best voice of the Occupation. Her stories not only frame her experience of those dark years; they also teach us to love, to forgive others, to be just and to strive for better than we have.

'Molly Bihet'
Paul Chambers
Fuji film

Naomi Taylor

Guernsey During My Life-Time

Naomi was five years old in 1940 when the Germans invaded.

'As a child it wasn't as bad as the adults' experience,' she recalls. The children weren't aware of all the complications that went on behind the scenes.

'In my case, my mum and gran often went without food to make sure I had something to eat.'

This is Naomi's story written in her school exercise book at the age of twelve, two years after the island was liberated.

Guernsey

Chapter 10

Guernsey During My Life-Time

In my life time things have altered a great deal. There has been the greatest World War ever known, Guernsey was effected a great deal.

There weren't so many boarding houses before the war as there are now. A lot of the big houses. There wasn't so much traffic as there is now. A few years before the Occupation there were no busses, there were all trams.

From 1940-1945 there was the biggest World War.

In 1940, the Germans invaded Guernsey. They landed here. When the Germans landed here, it was on a Sunday, we were in church, the minister went out to see what was happening, when he came back he said,

"The Germans have landed." When we got back home we saw a bus full of Germans going down the road, with tin helmets, guns, and gas masks. We were all very frightened, not knowing what was going to happen.

The Germans went into the houses of the evacuated people. After a little they put wire up to the windows. We used to laugh and say they looked like hens in hen houses.

They had a tremendous lot of fortification here. All under Delancey Park is hollow, it is all bunkers and tunnels. Under St Saviours Church it is hollow. There are bunkers and tunnels nearly all under Guernsey. When they were making a bunker on the Battery at the Red Lion, they had to blast. The stones were flying all over the place, one stone nearly killed my Gran. It fell right at her feet.

We had a hard time for food during the Occupation. One time we were three weeks' with out a slice of bread to eat. We had some horses' oats but they used to stick in our throats and nearly choke us. We fried the skins of the few potatoes we had and in linseed oil, they were awful. Some people say it was the pint of fresh milk the children had that kept them fit. Some times the Germans through a piece of bread out of the window for the rabbits, but the rabbits did not get it, it was us. But must people pulled through.

But the people who used to make us feel sorry were the prisoners who had to work for the Germans. Sometimes we would see them going on a long march, with a German with a gun in front and one at the back. Most of the prisoners had no shoes or socks. Their clothes were all ragged. If one of the prisoners lagged behind he was shot.

Many of the Germans were outwitted by Guernsey people. My cousin made himself a crystal set in a ~~thimble~~, but one day my Gran trod on it, by accident. So he made one in a match box, he took it to work with him in his pocket. My uncle kept his wireless in a box up in his bed room. Nobody in the family knew he had it. Some body told us they buried their wireless in the ground, when it was safe they dug it up again.

On May 8th 1945, it was Liberation Day. We listened to the crystal set and they announced us free. Everybody in Guernsey nearly went mad. Everybody was told they weren't allowed to fly their flags till 3 o'clock in the afternoon. People did not listen to that, most flags were out at 10 o'clock. When the Germans passed in their lorries they looked wild, the flags were flying in their faces. People were singing:-

"Don't fence me in."

The next morning, English soldiers came to Guernsey. People were crowding round them. Then a man with a recording car came, his name was Douglas Willis. He gave some chocolate to the children I had a bit. One young woman sang:-

"Sarnia Cherry Chérie"

Over the B.B.C. One I cannot really remember everything we were too excited

In the last two years, nearly everything has been put straight.

Marion Dorey

Hautes Capelles School Moves, 1941

Part way through my first term at school, one morning, a different teacher was waiting in our classroom.

'I'm Miss Veale', she announced. 'Your teacher Miss Barnett had to go away, so I'm going to teach you now.'

A simple explanation to cover the fact that Miss Barnett had been deported to a Labour camp in Germany because she was English, not local.

Miss Veale was a likeable teacher. Very soon we were used to her ways. A few weeks later Miss Veale gave us all a letter to take home. Mum read it and said,

'There will be no school for three weeks.'

'Oh, why can't I go to school?' I wailed, feeling very disappointed.

'The Germans want to use your school. There's nowhere to have school until another place is found.'

The Education Council arranged that some classes could use the Salvation Army Fortress at L'Islet. On the appointed day, Mum walked with my friend Pat and me to the new place. Our smiling Miss Veale was there greeting us and rounding up Standard I. That was a relief.

It seemed we had just learned the new route to school and started going on our own, when the Germans commandeered that building too. The next decision was to split up the school. Different classes would be held in private homes.

Miss Pattie Gaudion kindly offered two front rooms in her home Les Vieilles Salines to accommodate Standards I and II. This property had been a working farm. Encircled by tall elm trees, the present dwelling stood taller that its adjoining disused predecessor built of blue grey granite, with its small, square-paned windows peering through a mass of vibrant virginia creeper. Set apart from neighbouring cottages, Les Vieilles Salines was situated at the end of a curving drive bounded by a dry stone wall constructed of large, grey boulders, very characteristic of the walls along the rest of the lane. The main house had the traditional configuration of windows, five up and four down. Surrounding the immediate front of the house was euonymus hedging, enclosing a small area around the solid front door. The owner, Miss Pattie Gaudion, was very petite, dressed in long dark clothing of pre-war days. Sometimes we saw her walking along her drive. She appeared to conduct her life as if we weren't there, and never spoke to us.

The rules were simple. On arrival at school, those in Miss Veale's class entered the front door and turned right into the former dining room, now set up with desks for approximately twelve five and six year-olds. There was an inner door in the hall closing off the rest of the house, retaining its privacy.

Those in Standard II, Miss Evie Gaudion's class for seven and eight year-olds, turned left into the drawing room, with its Victorian black-leaded grate and beautiful patterned tiled surround. Usually a piano teacher, Miss Gaudion offered her services to the school as a teacher when other teachers evacuated.

When I was old enough to be in her class, I admired her brightly-coloured clothes and enjoyed the lively drama of her storytelling, her expressive way of reading poetry, and her rousing singing lessons, conducting us with the lift of an eyebrow while she played the piano. In other circumstances Miss Gaudion would have been a successful actress.

A typical day began with a hymn, some prayers and a bible story, then a spelling list to learn. Much of the work was oral, chanting tables, giving answers to mental arithmetic questions. I liked all the lessons with one exception, arithmetic. Placing the numbers neatly into ruled squares appealed. It was what to do with them afterwards that caused the difficulties. The sums that were correct were adorned with a lovely curly red 'R'. What I didn't like were those with an indelible red cross through them; a symbol of disapproval. When our sum book was complete it was to be taken home. My father would look through it. Had his sight and circumstances been different, he would have gone far in the mathematical world. I sensed a sadness about him at his only child's inability to grasp the principles of arithmetic.

After arithmetic came playtime. The so-called playground was bounded by the front hedge, the old stabling and 'not too near' the ancient wooden-gabled empty greenhouse with its reddish-purple paint now peeling for lack of attention. The other instruction was 'Don't go too far down the drive'.

We girls marked out houses, drawing lines with a twig to define the walls. We named the rooms where we pretended to be doing household tasks. For the most part the boys followed more energetic pursuits of chasing and fighting. We reprimanded them if they trespassed within the boundaries of our houses. On colder days we would run and skip and play tag to keep warm. The end of playtime was signalled with ringing of a hand bell whereupon we would line up in our classes and file back into the classrooms.

On bright days the sun streamed in through casement windows. When it was wet, the odour of damp clothing pervaded the area. If we were lucky enough to own a pair of Wellington boots, then we took a pair of slippers to change into. As the war progressed, our parents had to go to great lengths to obtain just one pair of shoes, quite often secondhand.

The premises were well-chosen. We all lived within about half a mile's radius from school. At dinner time we all scampered home for whatever nourishment our mothers had been ingenious enough to create from very little.

The teachers had a minimum of equipment and materials to use, so it was due to their imagination, ingenuity and dedication that their pupils made progress.

Trudie Shannon

Password

On the brow of the hill, the sentries stood
Armed, booted, helmeted, grey.
Standing every night
To stall and interrogate any one
Who cared to wend their weary way
Home toward the coast.
After curfew
On approach, they would demand, Halt and Password.

How she thought she knew that secret word
We will never know but one day
She claimed she did,
And her father dared to break the curfew confidently.

Returning beyond the witching hour
When soldiers trigger fingers twitched.
He saw the darker shadow shapes of men,
The glow of a lighted cigarette.
And though his heart pounded
He did not even engage the brakes,
Ignored the scuffling boots
And free wheeled by, shouting out the golden word
That Halt, Password superfluous for one in the know.
Unfortunately the word he shouted was simply that, a word
And not the word to allow safe passage.
When they shouted Halt in fiercer tones
He had already begun the hill's descent
The momentum of the incline sped him ever quicker.
So that the shots they fired into the night
Whizzed past his head quite harmlessly.
He lived.
How she thought she knew the password

We will never know,
But day by day
The weighted word was changed.
And she was unaware of that.

An Act Of Kindness

He was young, a mother's son
A reluctant soldier
She was sixteen, played the piano and accordion,
Sang like a linnet in concerts after curfew
Carried her accordion on her back.

Clothes were ragged by then, patches on patches
Homes were cold
They were hungry, all of them.
Chickens long gone, veg patch bare,
Cats just spooks in the shadows,
Cows and pigs figments of fantasy.
He was young, a mother's son
A reluctant soldier.

They never spoke just shared youthful glances
And one day when they were starving
She saw him leave a heel of bread upon their wall,
And she was overwhelmed by his kindness, his
selflessness
For she had seen his own gaunt features
His uniform hanging loose across bony shoulders
The shades of hunger in his own eyes.
He was just a boy, some mother's son
A reluctant soldier in a grey uniform.
She never knew his name, they never spoke.

Molly Harris

Writing on the Wall

In this painting the artist has employed part of the graffiti found on an interior wall of a German-built bunker.

The missing **'D'** and **'clear'** of **'Danger keep clear'** was entirely unintentional, but resulted in the phrase artwork reading **'Anger keep'**. This depicts the feelings of a devastated community in a despoiled landscape, which was originally painted on a tiny portion of Hitler's Atlantic Wall.

'Writing on the Wall'
Molly Harris
Acrylic
35CM X 43CM
*(By kind permission of
Rodney & Elmarie Brache)*

Richard Fleming

Outside Lloyds Bank

Outside Lloyds Bank, I pause because
I hear a sound that frightens me.
Approaching, jackboot-stamping feet
disrupt the day's tranquility
as, from the Pollet, upward come,
grey-uniformed, in rows of three,
stone-faced, the cold-eyed marching men
who stole our isle for Germany.
The little island, that we call
our Sarnia, has today become
a prison, where they dare install
their damnable Teutonic ways
but, fools they are, no Guernseyman,
with native stubbornness, obeys
such foreign laws, instead he mocks
their posters and communiqués.

They judge us fools, a lesser race.
Such arrogance to think us meek,
a servile race, our worth subsumed.
We bow and answer, tongue-in-cheek,
when challenged: subtle insolence,
mule-headedness, is our technique.
We will outlast them and survive
each angry day, each hungry week.
Fast-forward eight decades and see
the waving flags, a bright array
of finery and uniforms
as the parade goes on its way.
A different generation hails
those islanders of yesterday
whose boundless courage we recall
each year on Liberation Day.

PARADIS

I didn't think to
escape the pattern of my life,
to step sideways from this game.
It took someone to say I could,
though I knew that instant
that I should – so
I headed out
to amble
about,
to find
myself
here in
this lane.

Now I've
imagined a
land so vast
that lies beneath
an endless sky, a town
within from someone's mind
with roads that trace converging
lines to fields repeating rows of vines to meet
in timeless harmony, in symmetry as they designed.

But here,
another magic lies, in every
solitary house, in the separate
spirit of every tree, and the
gently waltzing
dappled light.
In a flash,
all sound goes.
I stop. I have seen

the house – its plain, clear
letters, quietly proud, spell PARADIS.

I stand,
a menhir
lost in time.
Behind stone
eyes, my mind
is veiled in fog of
childhood memory,
stories of sounds of
screaming carried far
across the parish, details
seen outside. How they knew,
with lowered eyes – but could not see.

Criminals can
scrabble to bury their tracks,
leaving little in the dust, as their world
closes in, then moves on. I know justice is
just an idea – but what a difference if kept? So
all know time can provide no final obscurity.
I have heard of hunters who did not forget,
and I begin to understand; where
shame is deficient, how humane
law should ensure such
perpetrators live
in fear.

As a seed scraped from a wall by a quiet wind,
I find myself walking away, through thickening
shadows under pines, up to a hill where
a warbler's
call carries

over fields
and flowers,
clear in the
last of the
evening light,
where I pause
in respect for
Marie Ozanne. And on and away I go, as a
bat circles round and loops back, the blue
sky brushed across with trailing cirrus lines.

Deep in the night I see the white horse, the
faint flash of a light at sea,
the yellow lamp,
the sentinel
cat's ears,
the broken
glass and orange
sun, the utter black of a
quarry's water cut by a bird, by its landing
wake. A gull calls, waters wash the shores. The
sheer granite drops deep, time's gravity
grows immense, the dream is
drawn down, and
disappears.

Pip Looijenga

Paradis

Pip was inspired by Nick's poem [see page 71]. She wanted to portray the house called Paradis in the Vale where much was heard, but nothing was seen.

On the day Pip visited Paradis it was bathed in beautiful sunlight which cast long shadows belying what may or may not have happened within those walls. In her black and white drawing of the house, the deep shadows add an eerie edge to the scene. Hidden in the picture are subtle hints to the alleged events, and the screams carried by the quiet wind.

'Paradis'
Pip Looijenga
Fine liner and acrylic paint
59CM X 42CM

Nicolas Rowe

Bulldoze through France.
Tread on our land.
Tell us the rules.
What must we grow?
Keep us apart.
Language will go.
Make us like you.
Drive things your way.
Dare us to speak.
Ration our food.
Leave us on bikes.
Let the old die.
Bring in your slaves.
Beat them when down.
Bring in your steel.
Build bunkers strong.
Set up your guns.
Lay out your mines.
Tower above.
Make us your fort.
Bully the Jews.
Threaten us all.
Devalue life.
Steal us on boats.
Send us to camps.
The airport's yours.
Stop all our boats.
Limit our post.
Telephones gone.
Now all alone.

Bomb from the blue.
Now you're the law.
What must we do?
Please tell us how.
Take over time.
Teach us your tongue.
Break in our house.
Pilfer the pound.
Curfew is here.
Take all the fuel.
Single file please.
Weakness is vice.
Let your slaves starve.
Torture them too.
Concrete our land.
Beaches are banned.
Lay your barbed wire.
Tunnel below.
Pen in with walls.
With slaves' lives bought.
Auschwitz for them.
Force us to work.
Throw us in jail.
Send us to France.
And eat our pets.
The harbour's yours.
Travelling gone.
Cameras gone.
Radios gone.
Now lost at sea.

Did you then think we'd cease to be?
We knew our hearts were always free.
Sarnia so dear. Sarnia Chérie.

Fortifications

Batteries and bunkers, blockhouses and watchtowers
Dotted like canker, inland and on the coast
Suppurating concrete blemishes to mar the eye,
To taint the rugged and the beautiful.
Clambering up overgrown steps to stand
Atop the concrete skeleton of a gun emplacement.
Its redundant tracking is revealed, exposing
Neglected teeth in rusting, graphic testimony to its past.
We are drawn to it, bidden invisibly and see that
With the passage of time
The track arc has become silently beautiful.
Rust blooms weep into the bald, decaying concrete.
While at our backs the sea glitters and seagulls sweep the skies
And in the distant haze, the vague outline of France.
Weighed with discomfiting memories of booming guns
That our generation do not possess, yet
Somehow catching like bile in our throats.
Somehow stirring emotions deep inside.

Chris Foss

Spaceship passing Fort Saumarez

Chris was born less than a year after the end of WW2 and these imposing structures made a lasting impression on him:

'The German fortifications in Guernsey were almost brand new when I was exploring them,' he recalls. 'I'd be quite scared because there'd be warning signs and barbed wire. They were crudely sealed and not too difficult to get into.'

These structures are a recurring theme in Chris' work:

'I'm fascinated by the proportions of the towers. They remind me of huge Easter Island gods looking out to sea. They're like big toothless masks.'

This is an extract taken from *Hardware : The Definitive SF Works of Chris Foss* by Chris Foss and Rian Hughes (Titan Books, 2011), reproduced with permission.

'Spaceship passing Fort Saumarez'
Chris Foss
Acrylic
46CM X 36CM
*(By kind permission of
Guernsey Museums & Galleries)*

Gilly Carr

Channel Islanders and the untold story of post-war PTSD

Our understanding of the occupation for almost every decade since 1945 has been shaped by the experience for ordinary islanders who endured military occupation coupled with that of German soldiers. While the experiences of those deported to the civilian internment camps of Biberach, Würzach, Laufen and Liebenau have become better known in recent years, our understanding of what happened to those deported to Nazi prisons, labour camps and concentration camps was almost unknown until very recently. While it had been established that a small handful of islanders were deported for acts of protest, defiance and resistance, the scale of these deportations had never been calculated. In fact, no comprehensive list of those sent away has ever been compiled by anybody – until now.

Funding from a Berlin foundation that sponsors academic projects on victims of Nazism enabled my construction of a website (www.frankfallaarchive.org), named after Guernseyman Frank Falla. Falla was a survivor of two Nazi prisons in Germany, where he was sent for his role on the Guernsey Underground News Service (GUNS). Another four of his colleagues were also deported, and two did not return. Having witnessed the death of other Channel Islanders in his Nazi prisons, Falla made it his business after the war to tell the families in Jersey and Guernsey the circumstances of the death of his friends. He was also responsible for helping islanders, who had been imprisoned in camps and prisons, get compensation in the 1960s, as victims of Nazism, from the West German government. Compensation was given to claimants on the basis of the amount of time they'd spent in a concentration camp or comparable institution and for the degree of disability they'd acquired as a result. Copies of these compensation testimonies in Falla's copious files, which his daughter gave to me in 2010, formed the basis of the resulting website. It was clear after whom the website should be named. This conviction was cemented after the discovery of enough clues in Falla's archive for me to work out, in 2016, the location of the final resting place of Falla's GUNS colleague, Joseph Gillingham, whose body had been lost since 1945.

The Frank Falla Archive website today lists the wartime story and prison trajectory of every single deported Channel Islander, as far as they can be reconstructed through archival sources from the UK, France, Germany, and the islands themselves. Original archival materials have also been placed online, providing the proof of the stories. The number of entries currently lies at 215, and these are joined by the profiles of the c.125 Nazi prisons and camps to which islanders were sent. We have no way of knowing whether or not we have reached the final figure of those deported, as crucial records on the continent were destroyed by the guards before the camps and prisons could be liberated. St-Lô prison in France, to which I calculate that at least 33 islanders were sent, was bombed by the Allies in 1944, destroying all records; lack of survival of crucial records has been a problem in calculating the final number of those deported.

Around three-quarters of the Frank Falla Archive's entrants' families have contacted me from the Channel Islands, the UK, as well as America, Canada, and Australia.

These family members have contributed stories, photos and further documentation to enhance the website.

In most cases, families did not know the full story of their deported parent or grandparent. Those who survived did not want to transmit the horrors of what they experienced to the next generation.

As families have contacted me, they have also quietly shared with me stories about the difficult behaviour of their loved one for decades after the war. These returning men and women often exhibited problems including strange eating habits, alcoholism, violence and aggression, withheld love, nightmares, anxiety, flashbacks, and loss of memory. These admissions were reflected in many of the testimonies written for compensation, of which I have now discovered around 100. In the testimonies, many islanders referred to suffering from conditions such as 'nervous diseases', 'nervous breakdowns', 'mental agonies' or a cluster of symptoms that today we would recognise as post-traumatic stress disorder (PTSD).

Although identified after WWI as 'shell-shock' or 'war neurosis', PTSD first began to be recognised as a syndrome in concentration camp survivors in the psychiatric literature in the 1950s and 60s, when it was known variously as 'concentration camp syndrome', 'Pathologie des Deportés' or 'Maladie de la Résistance', and was not fully understood. The introduction of PTSD as a diagnosis was recognised as a consequence of war, especially as something experienced by Vietnam veterans. Only in 1980, in the third edition of the authoritative *Diagnostic and Statistical Manual of Mental Disorders*, was it referred to as 'post-traumatic stress disorder'. This recognition helped to lift the stigma associated with the condition, and facilitated compensation claims in various countries, although this was many years too late to be of benefit to Channel Islanders.

Although such mental health issues were recognised in some European countries as having their origin in the camps, there is no evidence from their compensation claims that the various symptoms of Channel Islanders were diagnosed in this way. Not one of the testimonies uses terminology remotely approaching anything such as 'concentration camp syndrome' to describe their conditions, and only one uses the term 'psychoneurosis', a medical diagnosis.

This is likely to be an indication of how much English or Channel Islands' general practitioners, very few of whom would have experienced prisons and camps themselves, knew about the condition or were up to date on the mental health medical literature of this period. A diagnosis such as 'concentration camp syndrome' or similar would at least have had the benefit of acknowledging the cause of the symptoms, which would have allowed victims of Nazism to maintain their self-respect, rather than being thought 'mad', insane, or just odd.

In 1980, PTSD was defined by the American Psychiatric Association as something characterised by three groups of symptoms: those associated with reliving the trauma (such as nightmares or flashbacks); those related to avoiding any reminder of the trauma (such as memory loss, avoidance of certain situations, feelings of detachment and the loss of the capacity to express affection); and heightened irritability (including sleep disturbances, a quick temper and outbursts of anger). The symptoms of PTSD have since been added to, but many, if not all of these can be found in the testimonies of Channel Islanders. Because the disorder was not yet recognised and because the compensation claims form for disability did not encourage either physicians or applicants to ask or speak about mental health conditions, we have no means of judging whether islanders with some of these symptoms would be diagnosed with full PTSD today.

Of those who were deported, one of the more common problems described in compensation testimonies were recurring nightmares. Frank Falla was particularly explicit about these in his memoir *The Silent War*, writing that, after his return, he was worried about his health as he was 'experiencing severe sweats at night and the haunting hallucinations that I was back again in my prison cell at Naumburg … it was two hard years before I lost those night-sweats and hallucinations. I kept making noises and crying out in my restless sleep as though I was still in my cell…' Although Falla might have shaken off his night-time disturbances after two years, it was only in an interview following the publication of his 1967 memoirs that he revealed that 'I finally got the whole thing out of my system in this book'.

The trauma caused by the stress of deportation and imprisonment was too much for some. A few islanders lost their sanity following their incarcerations and spent the rest of their lives in and out of asylums. An example of this is Walter Dauny, deported from Jersey. Described as a 'small-time juvenile delinquent' and a teenager with a troubled home life, Dauny carried out a series of thefts of German property, and was deported to France in February 1944. He was sent first to St-Lô prison and then to Fort de Villeneuve Saint-Georges. As no record was found for him after the German withdrawal from France, it was assumed that he died in a concentration camp, and was subsequently named on the Lighthouse Memorial in Jersey and listed as one of the 'Jersey 22' (as the Jersey 21 was then).

However, in 2013 a nephew of Dauny's visited Jersey and saw his name on the memorial. He revealed that Walter was repatriated to the UK after France was liberated. In an interview he said that Walter did not die, but 'was terribly afflicted all his life as a result of his experiences in the camp'. He was in and out of hospital for tuberculosis, and asylums for his troubled mental health.

Given the number of islanders who seemed to be suffering symptoms of PTSD, of which those described here are just a tiny sample, it is interesting to note the lack of sympathy of the medical board whose task was to assess applicants for compensation. Frank Tuck, who stated that he had had several nervous breakdowns and was constantly having treatment for bad nerves, wrote in to make a complaint about the way that he was treated. 'I was appalled by the perfunctory nature of the interview … I was treated like an automaton, not allowed to speak except to answer the set questions put to me in a curt and cursory manner, and was completely unnerved. I do suffer from nervous disability and this was one of those days when I was particularly apprehensive … Everything about the atmosphere was cold, detached, impersonal and hurried. The whole exercise left an awful lot to be desired. From what I was told there by others undergoing periodical examinations, this pattern is not an unfamiliar one.' The medical board was, he complained, 'military-style' in its method of dealing with applicants.

If Tuck's experience of the official medical board was typical of that of other applicants – and there is no reason to think that they changed their method of assessment just for him – then it is concerning that those struggling with PTSD were not treated with more sympathy and care. In appears unlikely that the medical board had been briefed adequately about dealing with those with mental health issues arising from their wartime experiences.

The suggestion that PTSD was not a recognised disability as far as the Foreign Office, who administered the compensation claims, was concerned is reflected in their application form for compensation for disablement resulting from Nazi persecution. The questions on the form relate specifically to diseases and injuries and not to mental illness. After preliminary questions dealing with the patient's personal details, the form then asked claimants about the nature of the 'wound, injury or disease' for which they claimed. This is followed by questions asking where and how the wound or injury was inflicted, and when and where the disease began, and whether the applicant suffered from it before 'subjugation to Nazi persecution'.

Just one and a half lines were provided for details; scarcely enough space to detail even the physical injuries. Tuck, like others, was forced to squeeze text into the margins and outside the space provided.

Frank Tuck's example is extremely valuable in shining a light on a compensation system which did not take into account mental illness or psychological trauma caused by Nazi persecution. Not only were applicants not asked about this directly, but the system of assessing disability by medical board disadvantaged those with mental ill-health. Whether or not the doctors on the board asked applicants about psychological trauma is unknown, but it seems that applicants were not offered an opportunity to volunteer information if not first asked about it directly. The procedure was also clearly frightening and off-putting to nervous applicants who perhaps did not even consider their nightmares, anxiety, and emotional distress to be a 'disability' in the terms specified by the Foreign Office. Only those who were now confined to institutions stood a chance of compensation for their psychological suffering.

Patients were compensated on a scheme of percentage of disability. As those who claimed for disability compensation were affected physically by diseases such as tuberculosis, it is difficult to know precisely how doctors arrived at a percentage. What percentage, if any, did they award to those with serious mental ill-health but who were otherwise physically able to work and earn a living? Because mental illness was still stigmatised in the 1960s, it is probable that many (but not all) who suffered did not mention it, or marginalised its importance in their claim.

Without a doubt, symptoms of PTSD were common among surviving deported Channel Islanders and those symptoms often became chronic. Only a minority, it seemed, suffered no ill-effects at all – that we know of. Psychological symptoms ranged from nightmares and amnesia through to anger and a lack of emotion; others suffered nervous breakdowns and periods of complete loss of sanity. This behaviour went largely untreated unless it was extreme or obvious enough to warrant institutionalisation or urgent medical treatment. Otherwise, conditions were self-medicated with non-prescription 'tonics', alcohol, or managed through marriage to sympathetic and caring spouses.

The lack of formal treatment was probably due to a range of factors including stigmatisation of mental health issues, lack of affordability of this form of health care not then available on the National Health Service, and non-recognition of the necessity or availability of treatment, not to mention non-recognition of the condition itself. Brian O'Meara, for example, wrote in his testimony that he was 'able to recover completely' after Buchenwald. His children were able to attest to the contrary, stating that he had an explosive temper and was not affectionate or tactile with them.

Some of the deported men tried to channel their energies and experiences into something positive after the war, such as testifying at war crimes tribunals. Frank Tuck and his colleagues fought to clear their names through the Privy Council, as the offences for which they were deported were – astonishingly – not quashed after the war. Frank Falla helped as many islanders as he could claim compensation. These examples of strength of purpose and determination were from men who exhibited symptoms of PTSD and were affected by continuing ill-health. Inevitably, physical and mental health problems intervened on occasions – sometimes for extended periods – to prevent many islanders from working, from progressing in their careers, from supporting their families in the way that they might have liked, and from fighting for recognition. In fact, less than half of all deported islanders applied for compensation. Of those, 50% were successful, thanks to Frank Falla; this compares to a national average of a 22% success rate from the UK.

Yet why have the stories of those men and women who survived Nazi prisons and concentration camps not been part of occupation history for the last 75 years? Why is it not their memoirs that line the shelves of local bookshops? Why is Frank Falla one of the very few who wrote about their Nazi prison experiences? There's no simple answer to this, but PTSD in survivors certainly played a role, as did the physical injuries and diseases which plagued the remainder of the lives of survivors. Those who decided to become spokespeople were very small in number; the number of those deported in the first place was not large.

Acknowledging the mental and physical vulnerabilities of survivors allows us to understand the difficulties for them in telling their story. Recalling and reliving the brutality and violence of their imprisonment in order to recite their story – whether as censored versions for members of the family, or condensed for the purposes of compensation, or even repeated in detail for war crimes trials – would have re-traumatised the survivors with each retelling. It is not surprising that most never spoke of it again. This silence led to a lack of knowledge in families, very few written memoirs, and a lack of information with which to fill occupation museums, with the exception of a few notable cases. The Frank Falla Archive website breaks this silence and restores to the Channel Islands the last untold stories of the occupation. It speaks on behalf of victims and survivors and tells us what happened to the deported after the boats which removed them from their islands disappeared over the horizon.

~ ~ ~

Sections of this article are taken from Gilly Carr's latest book, *Victims of Nazi Persecution in the Channel Islands: A legitimate heritage?* (Bloomsbury Academic 2019).

'Remembering, Part 1'
Paul Chambers
Fuji film

Marion Dorey

1944-45

At the end of 1944, the population of Guernsey was feeling the effects of hunger. There was little food to be had. We were living in the Rue Sauvage, in the home of an evacuated family. One week, my father had called at Gibbs' grocery shop with our three ration books to collect our rations. All that was on offer that week was a small quantity of salt wrapped in a twist of paper, and one ounce each of cooking fat. He would later tell how he brought our supplies home for that week in his waistcoat pocket.

We in the country, with land to grow vegetables, had a supply of potatoes, parsnips and dried beans. Soup was on the menu most mealtimes. It was more difficult for people in Town, though some had friends and relatives who would supply them with a few things. Morale at that time must have been at an all-time low for the adults.

However, help was at hand. The Red Cross ship *Vega* brought food parcels.

The news spread round the island like wildfire. The parcels were stored at St George's Hall till distribution to the grocers could be arranged. They were guarded overnight by teams of local men on a shift system, though they had to remain on the premises all night because of curfew. They patrolled around the parcels for two-hour shifts.

Each family could collect their parcels from the shop where they were registered.

Queues quickly formed to collect them. This time Dad needed a small hand-cart to collect our parcels. When he arrived home our excitement was intense. Dad placed one parcel on the dining room table. At that moment nothing else mattered. This experience was being repeated in all the homes. The first parcels we received were of Canadian origin. The boxes were almost square, and made from very stout cardboard. A red cross adorned the sides, together with an address of origin. With a sharp knife, Dad carefully slit down the centerfold. He folded back two flaps, then raised the other two to reveal a series of tins of different shapes and sizes. One by one we lifted out the tins and examined them. A round yellow and brown tin was inscribed with the word 'Klim'. It took me ages to realise this was milk spelt backwards!

Powdered milk was a bit of a novelty, but had its uses, as did powdered egg. There was *Spam* meat, a tin of sardines, some thick, round, plain biscuits, butter and, I think, tea.

Real tea was so much nicer than the brews made of dried bramble leaves, dried peapods, or parsnip tops, which was all that was available then. But the most exciting tin to me was gold, and measured approximately four inches by six. When we broke the seal of that one, we discovered it contained chocolate, something we hadn't seen for ages. We just sat and gazed at all this. It was like finding treasure.

On another occasion we had New Zealand parcels. These were oblong, with a lid that could be lifted off completely. There were some variations in the contents. The powdered milk in this one came in a blue and yellow tin and was called *Cowbell*. It was not known how long the parcels had to last so we consumed one before starting on the others. The unopened parcels were kept locked away in case of burglars. At night time most families rigged up some sort of alarm system with wires, strings, tin cans, a handbell, or anything that would make a warning sound if there were intruders on the premises.

Around early February, we had our last loaf of bread. There was no more flour on the island. I remember my Mother giving me the last crust, saying she had no idea where the next one would come from. In fact, we were three weeks without any bread. My ninth birthday fell in that period. I don't think it was celebrated.

Then the *Vega* brought a cargo of flour. This was stored at Young's Mills near the Red Lion, and also had to be guarded by civilians. It was not available to the public, just to bakeries for bread. This bread was delicious, such a contrast to the rye flour used previously and had a bitter taste.

If we were hungry, it was much worse for the foreign prisoners of war living here in camps. They had to do forced labour, building defences. When they came begging, most islanders tried to give them something.

If the *Vega* had not come to our rescue during those dark days, many islanders would have reached the end of the line.

Nick Le Messurier

Twelve Bunches of Grapes

Emile thinks I'm mad.

'You'll risk your neck for a few bunches of grapes,' he says.

'Twelve bunches,' I say.

'What's going to happen if you catch somebody?'

'They'll run off.'

'They'll shoot you,' he says and, because he is better than me with words, he presses on. 'And then where will we be? Me and Alice, trying to run this bloody farm on our own.' He turns away. 'Think about that.'

I say nothing, which is what I often do when I'm losing an argument, but I know – and Emile knows – that nothing he says will change my mind. Alice says nothing as well, though she is not normally short of words. I think her heart agrees with me and her head agrees with Emile.

And so I'm sitting here in the greenhouse on two hay bales. A third bale is angled up behind me to make a sort of hay chaise longue; it's what we do when we're steaming through the night and trying to get a few minutes of sleep between shifts. But we haven't steamed for some time now, not since the Germans came, and the bales of hay are three years old. In the old days we'd use fresh bales and their sweet smell beneath you would help you snooze. Nothing's fresh now.

Except the grapes. Their smell is intoxicating. We kept only three vines and we have no sulphur to dust them

with this year, but in spite of that they have no mildew and are almost ready to pick. The smell. There is nothing like walking into a warm greenhouse and breathing in the scent of nearly ripe Cannon Hall grapes bunched on the vines.

It's getting dark. It's been a beautiful clear August day and the last smudge of light from the sun setting over Rocquaine Bay reflects on the greenhouse glass. The brightest stars are beginning to appear. The greenhouse is much cooler than during the heat of the day.

My hay bed is at the top end of the greenhouse, near the vines but not under them. Along the long rows, where tomato plants heavy with their fruit would have been three years ago, we are growing carrots and turnips – the potato crop has already been dug. The Germans tell us what to grow these days and in times like these, tomatoes are a luxury. There are no luxuries.

Except the grapes. A good crop. And this morning when we came into the greenhouse, one vine had been stripped of its riper bunches. Maybe six or seven. I'm still angry about it, though not as angry as I was first thing this morning. I count 12 bunches left.

'The bastards,' I say to Alice and Emile. 'They're not having any more.'

Alice looks at the branches which carried the heavy bunches the day before. 'I wonder why they didn't take the lot,' she says.

'Must have been only one thief,' Emile says. He's probably right.

The hay bales are comfortable enough. I have a whistle and a hammer and tin tray and I have a heavy stick next to me if things get difficult. I'm not afraid, not of an intruder. Words are the only things that scare me. My plan is that when the thief comes back, as he surely must, I will make such a din that he will think the bats from Hell are after him and run for it. He won't want to get in trouble with the Gestapo. They say that soldiers who break the rules are sent to the Russian front or, if it's serious enough, taken down to Petit Bôt and shot, but I've not met anyone who has seen it happen. The place is full of rumours.

When you don't have much food, you think about food all the time. People talk about food all the time, what they managed to get, how to make turnips and parsnips taste better, the prices on the black market – beyond most of us. We scorn those who would pay £30 for a pound of tea – how could they be so stupid – but we'd do the same if we had that much money to burn. Alice makes jam out of turnips and carrageen powder and raspberry cordial and we have parsnip pudding and cake made using potato peelings. How can Emile be surprised that I want to guard the grapes?

It's dark now, proper dark and well after the curfew. Apart from boys visiting their girlfriends the only people out and about now will be up to no good. It's getting colder and I cover myself with my heavy working coat. I'd be fine if I was moving around but I have to stay perfectly still. The weight of the coat is a comfort.

It is in my deep reverie, suspended between reality and the warmth of half sleep, that I hear the greenhouse door handle turn slowly and I think I can see the shadow of someone through the glass. It's difficult to be sure; your mind wants so much to see it – or not see it. But then the door opens slowly and I am certain. The hinges creak and there follows a moment when there is no sound. I keep still as the grave, not moving, not breathing, just looking to where I've put the hammer and tray. I feel the slight weight of the whistle hanging by a string around my neck.

After a moment that seems much longer than a moment I hear the door continue to open and a figure steps into the greenhouse. I let it come closer. I don't know why because the safest thing would be to create a God-Almighty din here and now, before the figure gets any closer and dangerous. But I want to see who it is. There is the creak of leather boots and I know it must be a German soldier, not a Todt worker – no-one else wears boots like those. I stay still, completely still, and the figure walks slowly and carefully down the centre path towards the vines and towards where I am sitting. More than a shadow now, he is a tall man, bare-headed, not carrying a rifle, but holding a wooden tomato basket. I can make out the bottom of his military jacket, which sticks out like a short skirt.

I wait until he is just a few yards away. And then I hear him unsheathe his bayonet. My heart jumps. Does he know I'm watching? Two quick steps and he could stab me in the chest before I could get up. Why did I let him get so close? I wait.

The shadow bends to put the tomato basket at his feet and then stretches his arm up to reach the first bunch of grapes. His other hand lifts the bayonet to cut the bunch from its branch. Carefully he bends again and places the full bunch in the basket. He moves a step and does the same again. I can hear his breathing.

And that's when I do it. I put the whistle up to my mouth and blow it as hard as I can. I crash the metal tray with the hammer, fast and furious, and the noise on that clear and silent night is enough to wake the dead. The thief's whole body jerks upwards, dropping the bayonet and the third stolen bunch of grapes on to the greenhouse floor. He staggers back and turns to make his escape, then drops to the earth, feeling around frantically for the bayonet. His hand finds the blade first, and he curses in pain. I don't stop my din – it seems to go on for minutes though in reality I expect it is for a few seconds. Without thinking, I get up and step closer towards him and for the first time I am aware that he can see me. I see his eyes and he sees mine.

He spits out a single syllable oath at me and I say, 'Go on, clear off!' I want to lay hands on him as he gets up but I know that this will take our confrontation to another level, much more dangerous. Instead I bang the tray even louder, holding it out towards him. He turns away, bayonet in hand, and runs along the path towards the door, stumbling into the soft earth either side whenever his foot leaves the compacted earth of the path. He half-falls against the door as he goes through it. I stop banging the tray and in the echoing silence that follows I swear I hear his footsteps running down the driveway and into the road.

I stand still, breathing deeply to try to relax, aware now how dangerous this meeting in the soft night has been.

I hear Alice's voice. 'John, are you all right? What's happened?'

We meet at the door and she hugs me tight, even though we are not a family that hugs. 'Did you scare them off?'

'You should have seen him go,' I say, and throw my head back and laugh, long and loud. 'You should have seen him go, the bastard.'

Emile is there now, standing next to us. 'I don't know what you're laughing at,' he says, 'You could have been killed. And all for a couple of bunches of grapes.'

He doesn't understand.

I stay in the greenhouse for the rest of the night but I am sure no other thief will be coming and I sleep deeply on the hay bales and under my coat. Early next morning Alice wakes me and we look at the scene. Here are the hay bales and on the floor of the greenhouse is the tray and hammer where I have left them. The whistle is still around my neck. The soldier's tomato basket, with two bunches of grapes carefully propped inside lies undisturbed on the path. A few feet away is a scattered bunch of grapes, some berries squashed, and close by on the dried earth is a trace of blood.

'He won't be in a hurry to come back,' I say.

'No, but others will,' Alice said. 'And some won't run away like he did.' She's right.

That morning we pick the remaining nine bunches from their vines. Four of them are turning from green to the beautiful yellow of full ripeness and the others are perhaps a week or two away. We take them all. For the rest of that day, Emile, Alice and I help ourselves to the berries from one bunch – the taste of the ripe grapes is so wonderful to tongues used to turnips, potatoes and parsnips that we can say nothing to each other as we roll the berries around our mouths. That evening, our stomachs, unused to such luxury, begin to grumble and over the next day the three of us spend more time in the toilet than ever.

We carry the box of grapes up the road and do a quick tour of the neighbouring families, giving a bunch to each household. 'If we give you more, you'll spend the rest of the day in the toilet,' Alice tells them. Most of us have nothing except their thanks to give us in return, but we do pick up a little butter, salt and flour.

The two least ripe bunches we decide not to give. We leave them in the box just inside the greenhouse door. A thief is welcome to them.

90

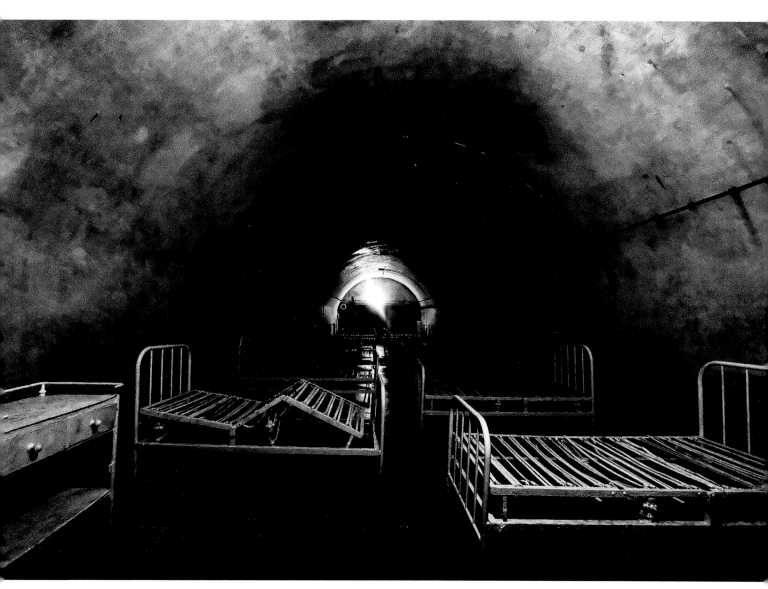

'Remembering, Part 2'
Paul Chambers
Fuji film

Rosanne Guille

Evelyn Guillemette's wartime cookery book

Evelyn Marjorie Robilliard, known as Queenie, was born in 1914. She was married to Louis Guillemette who was Secretary to the States Controlling Committee.

This little recipe book was shown to me whilst I was researching the food that Channel Islanders ate during the occupation, and I was delighted!

Queenie began writing out recipes in this recipe book in 1939, and she also stuck in a wonderful collection of cuttings from *The Star* newspaper. Some of the recipes show just how scarce food had become later in the occupation. I felt that the frayed and faded little book fitted perfectly with the title *In Living Memory*.

Louis and Queenie's eldest child, José, was born at Castel Hospital in 1942 and their life for the next three years was full of worry. 'My mother was a fantastic organiser and cook, and nothing was impossible for her, ever!' José recalled. After her mother's death in 2012, José inherited Queenie's cookery book. The book is still well used, particularly the Christmas pudding and apple chutney recipes.

'Evenlyn Guillemette's wartime
cookery book' (series)
Rosanne Guille
watercolour, actual size

Vegetarian pie
Lin Heing beans
Vegtables
Mashed potatoes

Line a pie dish with beans
add layers of vegetables
carrot + onions finishing
with a layer of meshed
potatoes. Bake until brown

Potato milk pudding

but up potato in small squares
(raw) add a little sugar
+ flavouring and milk and
bake in oven.

R Guille

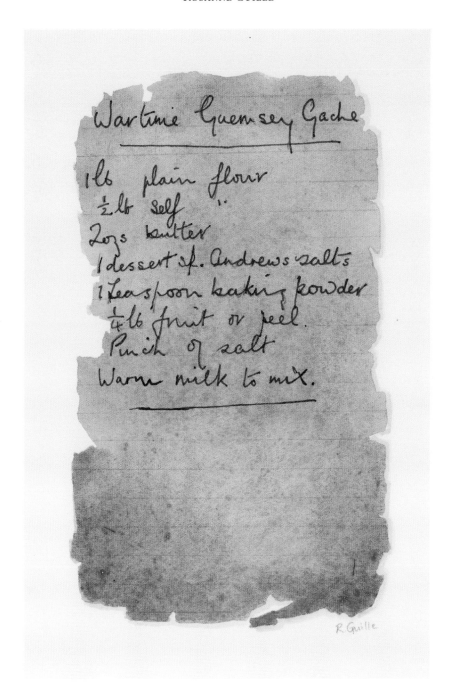

Wartime Guernsey Gache

1 lb plain flour
½ lb self "
2 ozs butter
1 dessert sp. Andrews salts
1 teaspoon baking powder
¼ lb fruit or peel.
Pinch of salt
Warm milk to mix.

R Guille

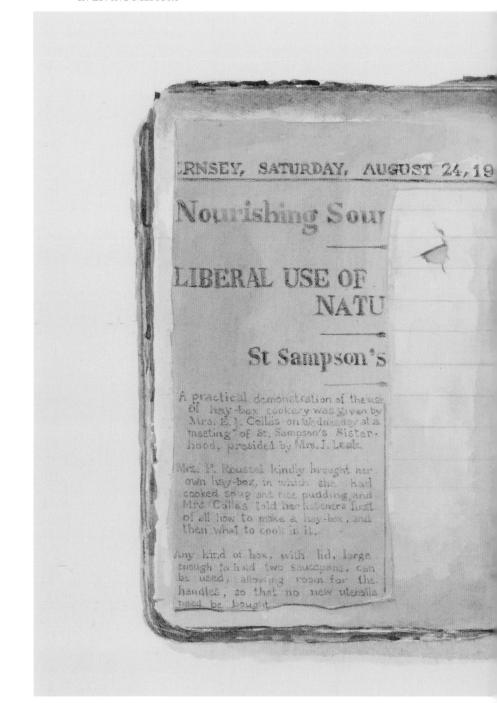

ERNSEY, SATURDAY, AUGUST 24, 19

Nourishing Sou

LIBERAL USE OF
NATU

St Sampson's

A practical demonstration of the use of hay-box cookery was given by Mrs. E. J. Collas on Wednesday at a meeting of St. Sampson's Sisterhood, presided by Mrs. J. Leale.

Mrs. P. Roussel kindly brought her own hay-box, in which she had cooked soup and rice pudding, and Mrs. Collas told her listeners first of all how to make a hay-box, and then what to cook in it.

Any kind of box, with lid, large enough to hold two saucepans, can be used, allowing room for the handles, so that no new utensils need be bought.

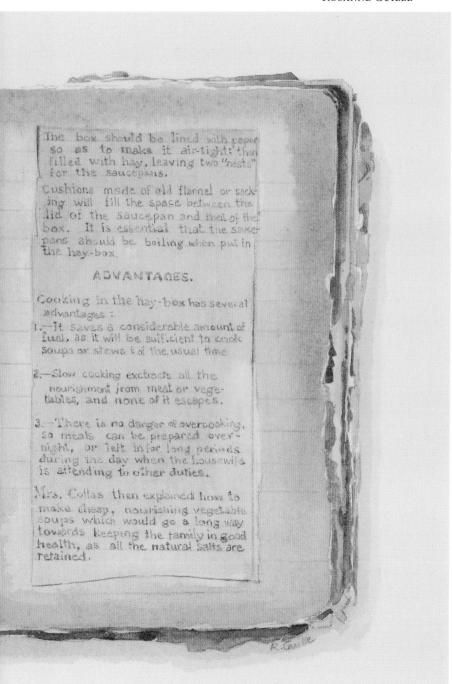

The box should be lined with paper so as to make it air-tight, then filled with hay, leaving two "nests" for the saucepans.

Cushions made of old flannel or sacking will fill the space between the lid of the saucepan and that of the box. It is essential that the saucepans should be boiling when put in the hay-box.

ADVANTAGES.

Cooking in the hay-box has several advantages :

1.—It saves a considerable amount of fuel, as it will be sufficient to cook soups or stews ⅓ of the usual time

2.—Slow cooking extracts all the nourishment from meat or vegetables, and none of it escapes.

3.—There is no danger of overcooking, so meals can be prepared overnight, or left in for long periods during the day when the housewife is attending to other duties.

Mrs. Collas then explained how to make cheap, nourishing vegetable soups which would go a long way towards keeping the family in good health, as all the natural salts are retained.

R. Guille

Marion Dorey

Preparations

In the short winter days of 1944, arriving home from school one cold afternoon I encountered an unfamiliar man just leaving through our back door. His parting words to my mother were

'I'll see you tomorrow morning then'.

My curiosity was aroused.

'Who was that, and why will you see him tomorrow morning?'

'That was Mr Quevatre. He's coming tomorrow morning to light our furze oven to cook meals for people in the area', replied Mum.

'Will he do ours too?'

At this point in the German Occupation, fuel was getting in very short supply. Gas and electricity were only available for certain hours in the day. Coal supplies were getting low. Many trees had been felled to supply wood for open fires, often used to boil kettles and saucepans, as well as to heat the room. The house we were living in at that time was owned by a family who had evacuated to England. In the corner of the scullery was a *terpid* and a furze oven, known in Guernsey French as *le grand four*. It had not been in use since we moved in.

Piled in readiness for the morning were a number of bundles of dried gorse or *furze*. This had been cut during the autumn with a special curved implement, then dried

out till it was almost colourless. In olden times furze would be sown into hedges to be cut annually so that a supply of fuel would be assured. The circular domed furze would be stored. It could then be conveniently dropped through the trap door when the oven was to be lit.

Next morning, we finished our meagre breakfast early to be ready for Mr Quevatre's arrival. I had never seen a furze oven lit, so hovered around expectantly before going to school. First Mr Quevatre cut open the bundles of furze and began to feed it into the oven with a furze fork, which was two-pronged, with a six foot handle. He ignited the furze, then pushed the burning material further back, constantly feeding in the bundles. I had to leave at this stage. As the heat intensified, the flame would burn white. It would take about half an hour to burn the furze to make sufficient heat for the bricks to get white hot. There was a tool to scrape out the resulting ash.

Earlier, people from the neighbourhood had brought their casserole dishes or bean jars, mostly containing previously-soaked dried beans and a bone with a little meat on it, flavoured with a few herbs, and a pinch of precious salt, which by now was almost unavailable.

When the ash had been raked out of the oven, these dishes would be placed inside, then the door sealed for several hours. At dinner time when I came home for some soup, there was an appetizing smell coming from the furze oven in the dark corner.

In former times, the family who owned this house would have had delicious meals baked in this oven, especially at Christmas and New Year, and at other times of family celebration. For more ordinary use, bread would be baked first, then levered out of the oven on a long-handled implement. The main meal of beef surrounded by potatoes, or *pornais à la graisse*, a dish of parsnips, soaked dried peas and port fat was cooked next. Finally Guernsey biscuits and apple dishes such as *gâche mêlaïe* and apple pies would be cooked in the diminishing heat.

Returning home after school, hunger pangs started to attack, with the now stronger aroma of cooking bean-jar. I amused myself with toys and a much read book until dusk came. It was a dull day, so dusk arrived early. At about quarter to five, the first person knocked on the door to collect her meal, then Mr Quevatre arrived. Mum invited them into the scullery. They were soon joined by others, some familiar faces, some unknown to me. It was strange seeing so many people in the normally empty scullery. Each person was clutching some kind of cloth or towel in which to wrap their dish, to contain the heat when they walked or cycled home. By now it was nearly dark. Mum lit a candle in the enamel candlestick and set it on the scullery table.

The scullery normally contained a table for working on, a sink with a cold water tap, a gas cooker, a cupboard for storing provisions and a haybox. This was made of a wooden crate lined with newspaper, then filled with hay. Ours contained two nests for saucepans. Mum would boil the saucepan on the gas for a short while, then put it in the haybox, close down the padded lid and the meal would continue to simmer for a few hours, thus saving scarce fuel. Today, however, the haybox was not in use.

There was general chatter in the scullery. Each arrival would make the candle flame flicker. Mr Quevatre was waiting for electric light. He couldn't see enough with a candle to take the dishes out of the oven. The electric light switch had been put on in anticipation. At five o'clock the light bulb received the power and illuminated the room. Those patiently waiting gave a cheer. The door of the furze oven was opened, releasing its heat into the chilly room. Mr Quevatre brought out the dishes one by one. Each was identified and claimed. Everyone could now go home to a much anticipated hot meal which would have an extra delicious flavour because it had been cooked in the furze oven. This experiment with communal cooking had also saved precious fuel.

Marion Dorey

The way I remember it

Happy, smiling crowds waved and cheered as the colourful noisy procession made its way from the Halfway to the Weighbridge on the afternoon of May 9th 1946. Lucky to get a good place, I was sitting on the sea wall at the Longstore with my parents. Crowds lined the wide pavement, looking expectantly towards St Sampson's. Union Jacks and red, white and blue rosettes were much in evidence. At ten years of age, I had never seen a cavalcade. In fact, I found the name rather fascinating. I like the fancy dress costumes, the penny farthing bikes, and recognised the ship *Vega* built on a float, carrying Red Cross parcel boxes. Even I didn't imagine that they still contained food. I knew only too well that the food had long since been consumed, though *Klim* and *Cowbell* tins were much in evidence in people's homes, once the powdered milk they had contained had been used. Some such domestic occupation themes were represented on the floats, along with evacuation scenes.

The naval band of HMS King George V led the procession. Overhead were low-flying aircraft piloted by the RAF, adding atmosphere to the occasion. The Home Secretary Mr Chuter Ede had come to the island earlier in the day to mark this very special occasion, the first anniversary of the Liberation Day.

Since May 9th, a year ago, life in the island had started to approach something resembling normality. Supplies of gas and electricity had been restored. Food was more plentiful, though still rationed. Radios had been returned to their owners. Cars and buses were back on the roads.

There bad been exciting family reunions when all the cousins had returned from the evacuation. School had returned to the Capelles building. Classrooms had become more crowded each week as more evacuated children returned. Strange and unfamiliar accents from Yorkshire and Glasgow could now be heard in the playground.

Now, on Liberation Day, the cavalcade noisily wound its way round the Salerie Corner and out of sight. The exhibits were to be judged at the Weighbridge.

It had all been so different on Wednesday, May 9th, 1945. I was then nine years old. I had awoken early in the unfamiliar attic bedroom where I had slept for the past two months since we had moved in with Gran'père. He was very ill and needed nursing. I looked out of the tiny gable-end window. It was a pleasant May morning. I lay awake for a while listening to the early bird song. Nothing so far indicated that this was to be an unusual day. Just then Mum came into my bedroom. Looking solemn and thoughtful, she sat on my bed, not a usual morning procedure. Mum explained that Gran'père had died during the night. Before going to bed I had stood just inside the doorway of his room and wished him 'Goodnight'. That would be my last memory of him.

I dressed and made my way downstairs. Breakfast was the usual milk sop. Mum then packed a few of my things in a bag and handed it to me. She said I was to go to my maternal grandparents, about a mile walk. She said there was to be no school that day. Soon I set off walking along the familiar route.

Caught up in the family bereavement, my parents had not explained to me that the war was officially over, and that the island was waiting for the British troops to land and free us. The Bailiff had made an announcement to the States to that effect yesterday afternoon.

This morning, the island was buzzing with news and rumours. The Guernsey grapevine was fully active jamming the telephone exchanges. My parents had been unable to warn my grandparents that I was coming to stay. Presumably they had wanted me out of the house before the nurse, doctor and undertaker would arrive.

My grandparents and the maiden aunts seemed mildly surprised by my arrival. When they discovered Gran'père had died, they said I would sleep there for a day or two.

After that, the aunts announced that we were going to Town. That was unusual. People didn't go there much these days. The shops were practically empty. We walked through Baubigny Road and came near the Halfway. A large ship was anchored outside the harbour. Lots of people were going to Town. Everyone was laughing and chattering. Flags were flapping from windows. Excitement was in the air. In Town, the White Rock area was still surrounded by barbed wire. Crowds of people gathered round the old harbour. The tide was out. At the harbour mouth was a ship. As we watched, the bows lowered to rest on the harbour bed. Soldiers laid down a roadway made of steel netting. When the roadway was laid as far as the granite slipway, lorryloads of soldiers drove out of the vessel onto this temporary roadway, up the slipway and on to the esplanade. The crowds were cheering, clapping, shouting to the soldiers and waving flags. Church bells were pealing in celebration. These khaki-clad soldiers threw cigarettes to the grown-ups and sweets and chocolate bars to the children.

I didn't catch any, but I didn't mind. I had enjoyed the chocolate in my Red Cross parcel that came in the *Vega* a few weeks before. Now everybody was talking excitedly about 'liberation'. I didn't know fully what it meant, but it seemed very special. Today had been proclaimed a public holiday.

After a while we went to stand outside the Royal Hotel where somebody called Brigadier Snow made a speech. People were trying to get his autograph. More British soldiers came marching to the Royal Hotel where they were to be based.

When all the excitement had died down we went back home to my grandparents to tell them about all the exciting happenings in Town.

The camp bed was made up for me. As I lay down I could not help thinking that one way and another it had been an eventful day. Gran'père had missed all the excitement. I found out later that he had known before he died that we were to be freed.

Liberation would be celebrated for many years to come, but no anniversary on it would ever be like this unique day in my life.

Mark Cook

Past Present Future

To commemorate seventy-five years since the liberation of Guernsey, the States of Guernsey has commissioned a permanent artwork which reflects the modern celebrations focused upon the activities of the day, whilst being respectful of the past.

These photographs are studies taken of the original master whilst it was still being worked upon in the studio before it was sent to England to be cast in bronze using the lost wax process. Each image displays different elements of the sculpture, which shows how textured form was used as a key element in defining the different materials conveyed within the bronze. The sculpture depicts a Guernsey family – signifying how the end of the occupation allowed families, torn apart by war, to return to the island reunited and how Liberation Day has now become a family celebration.

The male figure is wearing the uniform of the liberating troops, Force 135. This symbolizes both the original soldiers and also the re-enactors whose participation in the cavalcade and other events brings the period back to life.

The statue also contains other reminders of the immediate period following liberation, such as the chocolate bar, which represents those that were given out by the troops to the children after many hard years of food shortages and rationing.

The statue is designed to be interactive and stand at ground level, with the public being encouraged to form a physical link with the 'past and present' by holding the outstretched hands. Being at ground level also means it will become part of the crowds of people that throng the streets of St Peter Port throughout the day.

It is hoped that it will add to the public's understanding of the legacy of the war years by reflecting the positive and forward-thinking nature of the island since the end of the war.

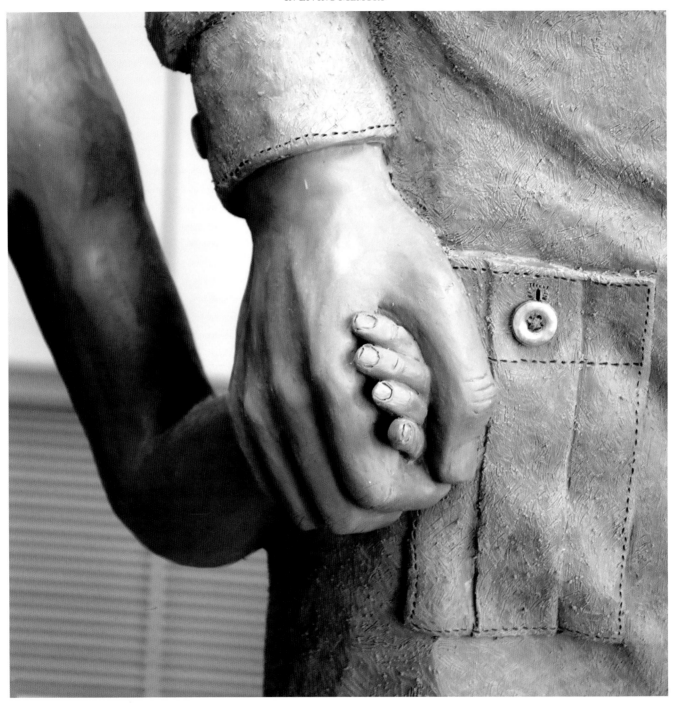

Annie Barrows

At the first Guernsey Literary Festival, in May 2011, Annie Barrows, co-author, with her aunt Mary Ann Shaffer, of 'The Guernsey Literary and Potato Peel Pie Society', spoke at a dinner celebrating the occasion. The following is an excerpt from her remarks that night.

Recently, I shuffled through my files and discovered that I have, since the publication of *The Guernsey Literary and Potato Peel Pie Society* three years ago, given 122 talks about the book, about Guernsey, and about the island's occupation during the war. I've been on panels, I've been filmed, I've been interviewed, I've spoken before thousands of people, I've even judged potato peel pie contests. But the prospect of speaking before you tonight nearly struck me dumb. I could not imagine what I could say to you that would not be presumptuous.

When I first began to work on *Guernsey Literary*, I worried a great deal about presumption. Was it presumptuous of me, an outsider, an outlander, to write about the wartime experiences of the people of Guernsey? Was it morally suspect? Was it effrontery? I fretted about these issues for some time, and then I said to myself: men have been writing about women for centuries, and they certainly aren't losing any sleep over it. That made me feel better, but I began to fret once again when I thought about this evening. For while I do not think it was presumptuous of us to write about the occupation, I think it would be horribly arrogant of me to stand up here and tell you what the occupation meant, either in general or to you.

What I can tell you, however, is what your wartime experiences have come to mean to readers of *The Guernsey Literary and Potato Peel Pie Society*.

My aunt Mary Ann Shaffer's lifelong dream was to 'write a book that someone would like enough to want to publish'. When the manuscript of *Guernsey Literary* found a home with the Dial Press in the United States, it was the fulfilment of that dream. Soon enough, we began to feel that the book was not merely going to be published, it was going to be a success. We could tell, from the early reviews, from our publisher's excitement, from the interest in other countries, that our book was destined to do fairly well. Our belief that *Guernsey Literary* would be a testament to Mary Ann's talent was a comfort to my family when she passed away five months before it was published.

So – we were prepared for a success. We were not prepared for what actually happened. The book was published and immediately climbed up the international bestseller charts. This was very nice indeed, but what transcended its performance on the charts was the outpouring of emotion from its readership. Everyone who read it seemed to take it to heart. It's true that readers are passionate in their affections, but this went beyond anything I'd seen before: people sat in the audience at my readings, weeping. They wrote me letters begging for more, more, more story, a sequel, an anything. Books mean different things to different people, and many people were responding to Elizabeth and her fate, to the love story of Dawsey and Juliet, to the wryness that seems to have been a peculiar strength of the British people during the war. But a sizable group found another kind of meaning in the book, one that was derived from the unique situation that occurred in Guernsey: the intense, daily, inevitable interaction between islanders and invaders for nearly five years. On an island, starving together. In the book – and, I believe, in reality – the definition of one's 'enemy' becomes blurred or at least intermittent under these circumstances. It becomes difficult to see a monolithic Enemy; time and experience replace the unequivocal category with the possibility – and perhaps necessity – of individual assessments and even friendships. This ambiguity made a striking impression on some readers.

For example, at a panel discussion in Nevada, a native Chilean recounted his experiences growing up in Chile as Pinochet overthrew Allende. In his family, he said, there were supporters of Allende and supporters of Pinochet, and the division between them was so virulent that it split them apart. Each side felt that if you weren't for them, you were against them: black or white, yes or no. The end of Pinochet had not brought about an end to the conflict, he said. There were members of his family who had not spoken for years. What he saw in *Guernsey Literary* was an example of greyness, a non-categorical possibility, a maybe-ness that could, perhaps, open the door to reconciliation. So he sent copies to all his cousins – and they refused to read it.

In another instance, a German teenager wrote me the following, 'As you might guess, it is not always easy for us (German youth) to read literature concerning the Nazi regime, as we haven't quite figured out how to deal with the guilt that is being passed on from generation to generation. Still I felt that in *Guernsey Literary and Potato Peel Pie Society* someone had found the right tone, the right words to describe what I haven't experienced myself but what I have to deal with every minute of my life. I read about all the horrors Elizabeth had to go through at Ravensbruck, and I did not feel like a criminal afterwards.

This might not seem special to you, but for me it was an amazing experience.'

Even a Guernsey islander, who'd been deported to a German concentration camp during the war, felt that the book allowed him to be included in the events of his community in a way that had been denied him before.

It is, however, the response of my own countrymen I find most hopeful. Given the American reputation for historical ignorance, I'm sure no one will be surprised to hear that hundreds – okay, thousands – of US readers learned for the first time about the occupation when they read *The Guernsey Literary and Potato Peel Pie Society*. And the island has fired their imaginations. I get letters, hundreds of letters, from readers who want to come to Guernsey to see where it all happened; they want to see the bunkers and gun-turrets, to see St Peter Port, the beaches, the views, the little roads. Some of them want to meet poetical pig farmers. Go, I reply, go now! They should come here, not simply to see the sights, lovely as they are, but because there is something Americans need to learn from Guernsey. As citizens of the most warlike nation on earth, we are very, very good at defining our enemies and very, very bad at living with them. Your history offers us a model for seeing beyond the division, for looking beneath the label, that we desperately need. From you we can perhaps learn to become a better enemy, which is the beginning of becoming a friend.

This is why tonight is an opportunity, not for me to say what your wartime experiences mean to you, but to thank you for what they continue to mean to the rest of us.

Frances Lemmon

The Last Alderney Cow

The oil painting, 'The last Alderney Cow', is the latest in a long line of visual stories worked on by Frances Lemmon.

The Alderney breed of cattle was renowned for its rich creamy milk which made excellent butter.

In the summer of 1940, after the majority of islanders had evacuated, a party of men were sent from Guernsey to retrieve the cattle. However, once in Guernsey, the cattle were interbred with local breeds.

A small number of pure-bred Alderneys remained on the island, but these were killed and eaten by starving German troops in 1944. As a result, this unique breed died out.

Frances comments: 'The joy of using an animal rather than a person as your central character is that you can be more oblique with your meanings. There was a lot of anguish in Alderney ... the cow represents all those people that were taken to the island and never left.'

'The Last Alderney Cow'
Frances Lemmon
Oil on canvas
61CM X 52CM

Karen Simpson

Five long years

When the boats came, we had two hours to pack our life.
My ancestors had farmed this strip since medieval times.
We took the dog to the butcher and his body was added to the bloody pile
but we didn't tell the children.

One suitcase each and we didn't lock the door.
My invalid mother was carried down the hill but the children thought it was an adventure and they laughed as their childhood was captured in one last photograph.

The chatter didn't drown the distant guns;
they were close.

The island disappearing into the gloom was imprinted on my mind, 'à bétao' I whispered to myself.
The crossing was rough and we were squashed in more than the boat was meant for; we were scared.
When we arrived at the port the local people were kind; they gave us food and blankets and we rested.
We finally made it to our new home; they had got a translator but we talked their language and the unaccompanied children lined up to be chosen.

Five long years we stayed.
Our children grew up forgetting their language, their heritage; they became locals.
They cried when it was time to go back to a distant memory of a forgotten childhood.

Our house was a shell; to keep warm they had burnt our furniture and wooden door frames.
Only walls stood.

We had nothing.

They had kept the best furniture so it was brought out into a field and we fought off our friends to take what wasn't ours.
Embarrassed – we closed our doors to the neighbours that day

Everything that defined us was gone.
Forgiveness did not come easily.
Lest we forget

Taken from a conversation with Olympia and written as a monologue in his own words.

In June 1945, when I was just five years old, my family were evacuated from Alderney. We arrived in Weymouth and then travelled by train to Glasgow. After two weeks, decisions were made depending on our father's trade, my Dad was a farmer, so we were sent down to Wiltshire. We stayed there for the duration of the war, until December 1945.

My twin brother, Nick, and I went to the local village school. We were the only Channel Island family there. My dad was the head herdsman for a big dairy herd and we were given a cottage on the farm, so we had somewhere to live too. It was a tithed cottage. It was comfortable enough. We all seemed happy with it all. Sometimes we thought it was a big adventure, you know, my twin brother and I. And being a small village it almost felt like living in Alderney. The school there was the same as back home, a small mixed school and you had all your pals there together in one class.

We stayed a bit longer after the end of the war and were on the first boat back to Alderney on 15th December 1945. When we arrived we went to see our family home. Well the roof was still on at least! But there were no doors and all the sliding sash windows were gone, it was just the wooden frames left in the stone work. There was no furniture, empty rooms and five years of dust and muck. It was derelict really.

We were given four days to get it habitable. We had help from the German prisoners of war. They put what we used to call window light – a thick plastic sheeting that was reinforced with strands of wire in it, big rolls of the stuff – and you just nailed that over the openings. They put a front door and a back door and then we had to start cleaning, because everything had been covered in that insecticide stuff, DDT. We didn't know what it was.

We were all issued with a bed, it was a military-style camp bed, a chair and a Canadian handmade bedspread, quilt thing, from the Red Cross. So a pretty basic start.

That first Christmas we had this little meat ration. I don't know where my Dad got hold of it, probably through one of the farmers, but there was also roast rabbit for Christmas table. I don't know how my mother did it sometimes.

My twin brother and myself – we had appetites you know. It always made me wonder how they managed during the war with all that rationing. Somebody said we had the best diet going when we were growing up. Everything was homegrown and homemade, you weren't overly fed and that's why we're all so lean and fit.

I was ten-and-a-half years old when we came back December 1945. We had no school until the September of the following year. Nine months of no school and there were big guns out there on the cliffs – the big range-finders were working, and where the airport is now it was all trenches and you could go from bunker to bunker. One lad blew his fingers off. There were mine detonators and he'd taken the cap off with a pair of scissors – it blew his thumb and half his finger off. You couldn't keep us kids away from all that could you!

My parents had my younger brother, Fiff, to look after, so us twins went off playing. Mind you, we all had to work three days a week digging up potatoes that winter. The Germans had planted up the fields the previous year, so in February and March it was time to dig them all up. It was a communal farm and there were girls working there as well. We were ten-and-a-half, eleven years old working three days a week. The German prisoners of war were there and there was only one old tractor on the island. There was also a horse and plough, so they'd go along turning the ridge of potatoes and we had to go along with our bare hands putting them in buckets and then into sacks.

Think about it, February and March, those cold easterly winds, we were frozen because we had no protective clothing like you have these days. We had an old pair of overalls and an old sports jacket tied up with string and that was it.

All those potatoes from the communal farm went into the only shop on the island. Everything was rationed. There were also a few pigs on the go for meat production and they got some of the potatoes for feed too. After that first summer we got our own land back. It was a big garden and we grew our own vegetables, otherwise we'd have gone without.

That communal farm didn't last long. People got fed up with it – they wanted to go back to the way they used to live. The communal farm was a bit too much like communism, that's what the old folk used to say. Quite a few men had their own little farms before the war and then to be thrown into something bigger like that, it didn't work. Prewar all the land was laid out with dry stone walling – it was very much like Normandy farming and the families had their own strips here, there and everywhere. They were used to having their own little farms and that was all gone when they got back after the war. All that dry stone walling had probably gone into those bunkers.

All the boundaries for the farms had gone, so some of the British Government and Land Commission found some old records and it was all marked out again, and new maps drawn up, and everybody got their bit of land back.

So we probably had the POWs working for us for two or three months on and off – it wasn't every day of the week. You'd have a carpenter come in and he'd put the doors on the bedrooms and a week later somebody else would come in and put skirting boards back. The one thing the Germans had done for some, even though the houses were left derelict, they put in running water and electricity. There were quite a lot of properties on the outskirts of the island that never had electricity or running water before the war. There was destruction on one hand but there was something good that came out of it on the other.

The German prisoners did have some good craftsman. It was all part of the rehabilitation scheme that the British

Government had brought in. Because at the end of the war Alderney was in such a mess the British Government said nobody was going back. They were going to use the island for training grounds for the British army, once all the mines were cleared.

Our Homecoming was hard for all of us. There was a lot of work to be done. But they were good times and we made the best of everything. We made new friends again, but the only trouble was, we couldn't understand each other. All those broad accents. Us twins with our Wiltshire, my cousin with his broad Devon, and then there were Scottish, Yorkshire… All different accents!

When we started back at school the following September, all the teachers from before had gone, so we had a new set of teachers and a new school. In the first year there were only two big classrooms, mixed boys and girls, and then one other building for the youngsters, five to eight years old. I was in the last year when the school leaving age was fourteen. And that's when my working adult life began.

Below: Peter with his brother Nick and a friend on board the first returning boat (the Autocarrier) approaching Alderney on 15 December 1945

Olympia McEwan

Homecomer story, dedicated to Beda

Beda Thompson's portrait represents the story of the Homecomers of Alderney. Beda, her sister and their mother and father, fled the island in 1940 along with all but seven of Alderney's residents.

She had mixed feelings about their Homecoming Day in December 1945:

'I was very happy to come home but sad to see the state of the island. Some people saw it, turned around and never came back.'

But she and her parents' generation were determined to stay, in order to rebuild their lives and their precious island home.

Beda Thompson died before the portrait was completed, so it is now dedicated to her.

'Homecomer story,
dedicated to Beda'
Olympia McEwan
Mixed media
113CM X 75CM

Profiles of Contributors

Survivors

Ethel Brouard (née Le Noury)
Ethel was born in Guernsey and was evacuated with her school to England. Ethel was a coordinator of an initiative to collect the stories of those who came home to family ties which had been broken, and in some cases never recovered. Ethel's survivor story is her essay, 'A Child Apart', which she wrote for this project.

Marion Dorey (née Robins)
Marion was born in Guernsey and recalls her memorable stories in four beautifully-written essays, none of which have been published before. It is a great honour to have them included in the pages of this book.

Shirley Falla (née McCarthy)
Shirley was very young during the occupation of Guernsey, but still remembers some of her wartime experiences with real clarity.

Peter Gaudion
Peter and his family were evacuated with all but seven of the entire population of Alderney. Their evacuation experience was a happy one. They lived on a farm for the duration of the war. Their homecoming was rather brutal, with a derelict home to repair and their livelihoods to rebuild.

Margaret Le Conte
Margaret was sent away from Guernsey with her school during the occupation. Her story is of upheaval and homelessness at the beginning of the war years, but settling finally in one place with both her mother and brother, recalling her happiest and sometimes most terrifying experiences, in her conversation with Olympia.

Mavis Lemon (née Wakley)
Mavis was born in Sark and lived there throughout the occupation years. She now lives in Guernsey and will be celebrating her 90th birthday this year. She was kind enough to meet with Olympia to talk about her war time memories, which are included in this book, in a monologue-style essay.

Diana Nicole (ex De La Rue, née Bachmann)
Diana is an author and charity campaigner. She has had an extraordinary life beginning with her evacuation from Guernsey to England, during WW2. She recounts her memories most vividly in her essay, *The Emotional Severance*.

Janet de Santos (née Duquemin)
Janet was eighteen months old when she and her mother were deported from Guernsey. Her mother was an Austrian Jew. Their story is a survivor story of the civilian internment camp of Biberach, in Germany, where many Channel Islanders were sent.

Naomi Taylor (née Keyho)
Naomi has lived in England for most of her life. She was born in Guernsey and has recorded her childhood memories of the German Occupation in a heartfelt essay, handwritten when she was just twelve years old, published in this book for the first time.

Artists

Paul Chambers

Paul studied fine art at Cheltenham College of Art in the late 80s and explored photojournalism with the Amos Trust and Christian Aid in Ghana, Tanzania and Palestine in the 00's. A curious traveller and former doctor of trees; Paul found himself leading an Ecumenical community in Guernsey for ten years before moving on to working in the Criminal Justice System for another decade developing Restorative Practices. He now approaches his half century and has become a full-time photographer, exploring the next chapter of his life with all the creative opportunities it promises.

Mark Cook

Mark Cook has created artworks both commercially and professionally, spanning both 2D and 3D mediums. 'Past, Present, Future' is his latest piece of public art and will be unveiled as part of the official States of Guernsey's 75th celebrations of the liberation. As a painter he has been commissioned to create various portraits. His work can be seen in private and public collections in both the UK and Guernsey. He has had three pieces of work exhibited in the National Portrait Gallery in London.

Chris Foss

Chris Foss first experimented with airbrushes in the early 60s and has become one of the most widely-recognised artists using this medium. He has created over a thousand book cover artworks for authors such as Isaac Asimov, E. E. Doc Smith, Arthur C. Clarke, A. E. Van Vogt and Philip K. Dick and many others. He has also worked in film design on *Dune*, *Superman*, *Alien*, *Flash Gordon*, Stanley Kubrick's *A.I.* and Marvel's *Guardians of the Galaxy* released in 2014. More recently he was at Ealing Studios, London, working with Black Mirror.
www.chrisfossart.com

Rosanne Guille

Rosanne Guille grew up on the tiny Channel Island of Sark and went on to train in Natural History Illustration and ecological studies at Bournemouth and at the Royal College of Art. Her paintings have been shown widely in exhibitions including the Society of Wildlife Artists and the Royal Miniature Society and she has illustrated for publications such as Usborne books and BBC Wildlife magazine. She is a member of the Artists for Nature Foundation and was the organizer of their Jubilee project 'Art for the Love of Sark' in 2011/12. Rosie now lives and paints in Guernsey.
www.coachhousegallery.gg/artists/guille-rosanne

Molly Harris

Molly Harris was born in Guernsey in 1946 and in 1952 moved with her family to live in the Scottish Borders. From 1961 to 1964 she attended the Carlisle College of Art, Cumbria, where she studied graphic design and related subjects.
In 1964, she enrolled at the Edinburgh College of Art to study mural painting, graduating in 1966 with a diploma in drawing and painting. She then taught in colleges in Manchester, before moving back to Guernsey in 1969. She stopped painting at this time and did not resume until 1982. The following year saw her first exhibition at the Coach-house Gallery.
In 1986, she had an exhibition at the Paperwork's Gallery in Vancouver Canada, and her work has also been shown at the Pike Gallery in St John's Wood London.

Frances Lemmon

Frances trained at London College of Printing, Sir John Cass school of drawing and Camberwell School of Art in the 1980's before working as a scenic artist and faux finisher in London and New Zealand, returning to live in Guernsey in 2002.
www.franceslemmon.com

Pip Looijenga

Pip Looijenga is a local artist and illustrator. Pip studied art as a mature student at the Guernsey College of Further Education and in 2019 was awarded a Distinction on her Extended Diploma in Art & Design course. Pip's work can be seen in various galleries on the island, including Iris & Dora, Framecraft at the Coach House Gallery and Sula Gallery. Pip was inspired to create her piece in response to Nicholas Rowe's poem 'Paradis'.

Olympia McEwan

Olympia is the curator of this book. Her vision was to use original material, most of which has never been shared or published before. As an artist living and working in Guernsey, she has exhibited in several shows, with her work in private collections around the world. Olympia continues to have a keen interest in portraiture: 'I am a storyteller in pigment and paint'. Stories such as her *Amazing Women* in 2018, in which she created 15 paintings of women making a difference in our island community. *Trailblazer* is her forthcoming show, celebrating further stories of women of Guernsey, who are making an impact in their various fields.
www.olympiamcewan.com

Writers & Poets

Annie Barrows

Annie Barrows is a well-known author of children's books, including the *Ivy and Bean* series and *The Best of Iggy*. *The Guernsey Literary and Potato Peel Pie Society*, which she co-authored with her aunt Mary Ann Shaffer, was published by Bloomsbury in 2008. A *New York Times* best-seller, it has been published in 37 countries and 32 languages.
Annie lives in Northern California with her husband and two daughters.
www.anniebarrows.com

Jeni Snell

Jeni Snell (born 1972 in Guernsey) graduated in 2007 from Central Saint Martins College of Art and Design with an MA (Fine Art) and in 1999, with a First Class BA (Hons) Fine Art in 1999 from the University of Sunderland. She lives and works in London.
www.jenisnellart.co.uk

Siân Jones

Siân Jones (born 1986 in Guernsey), graduated from the Arts University Bournemouth in 2012 with a BA (Hons) in Fine Art. Jones' practice explores questions of identity, gender and sexuality and how society's reaction to these affect our mental health. The main aim of Jones' work is to provide a platform for discussion and raise awareness by publicly exhibiting her work as street signs or paintings.
www.sianjonesart.co.uk

Ryan Morley

Born in the Lincoln Wolds, Ryan has been a Graphic Designer and a creator of visual installations for over 20 years. He moved to the Channel Islands two years ago practicing in design and lecturing in Art & Design at the College of Further Education.
www.birdandbee.co.uk

Gilly Carr

Dr Gilly Carr is a Senior Lecturer and Academic Director in Archaeology at the University of Cambridge. She is also a Fellow of St Catharine's College, Cambridge, a Fellow of the Society of Antiquaries, and a Fellow of the Royal Historical Society. Gilly has over 65 publications in the fields of Archaeology, Heritage Studies, History, and Holocaust Studies. She is the Channel Islands representative on the International Holocaust Remembrance Alliance.
www.frankfallaarchive.org

Richard Fleming

Richard Fleming is an Ulster-born poet and short story writer resident in Guernsey. His work has been broadcast and widely published and will be familiar to listeners of BBC Radio Guernsey. He has two poetry collections currently in print: *A Guernsey Double*, in collaboration with UK poet, Peter Kenny and *Stone Witness*, recently published by Blue Ormer. www.redhandwriter.blogspot.com

Richard Guille

Richard Guille is a PhD candidate at the University of Kent. His research examines the subjective construction of personal testimonies of the German Occupation of the Channel Islands, utilising oral history as his primary research methodology. His broader research interests include modern British history and oral history theory and practice.

Nick Le Messurier

Born to Guernsey-French-speaking parents, writer Nick Le Messurier worked as a local journalist and teacher of English. Now he writes. Nick's fictional story is based on something his mother told him and his brothers – both parents were in Guernsey during the occupation. 'They did sometimes talk to us as children about the occupation, but it was only later we learned how tough things really were.'

Nicholas Rowe

Nicholas Rowe's grandparents have been a major inspiration to him, especially for this project. His great-grandparents in Guernsey were deported to Germany for refusing to run their vinery for the Germans. His maternal grandmother, Miriam Mahy, is the author of *There is an Occupation...* Nicholas holds her as a great example of humanity despite her life experiences. He set himself a goal in late 2017 to become a writer in order to use his creativity, and to be able to move and inspire people. He wrote his first poem for over twenty years, set up his poetry blog, and now feels very honoured to be a part of *In Living Memory*. www.nickrowepoetry.rocks

Trudie Shannon

Trudie Shannon is an artist and poet, born and raised in Guernsey. She had her first collection of poetry published aged twenty-six. Her muse is her environment and the people she encounters within it, often writing as if she were in that person's shoes. She has co-edited two collections of local poets work *One Wing* and *Another Wing* and performed her work both on and off the island, participating in Open Mic nights over many years and guesting on BBC Radio Guernsey a number of times. guernseypoets.blogspot.com

Karen Simpson

Karen Simpson is a local science teacher and cub leader who enjoys both writing poems and children's stories based around and about the Bailiwick of Guernsey. Her parents were children during the second world war, so she is very interested in learning about the history and heritage of the islands.